Outrageous Fortune

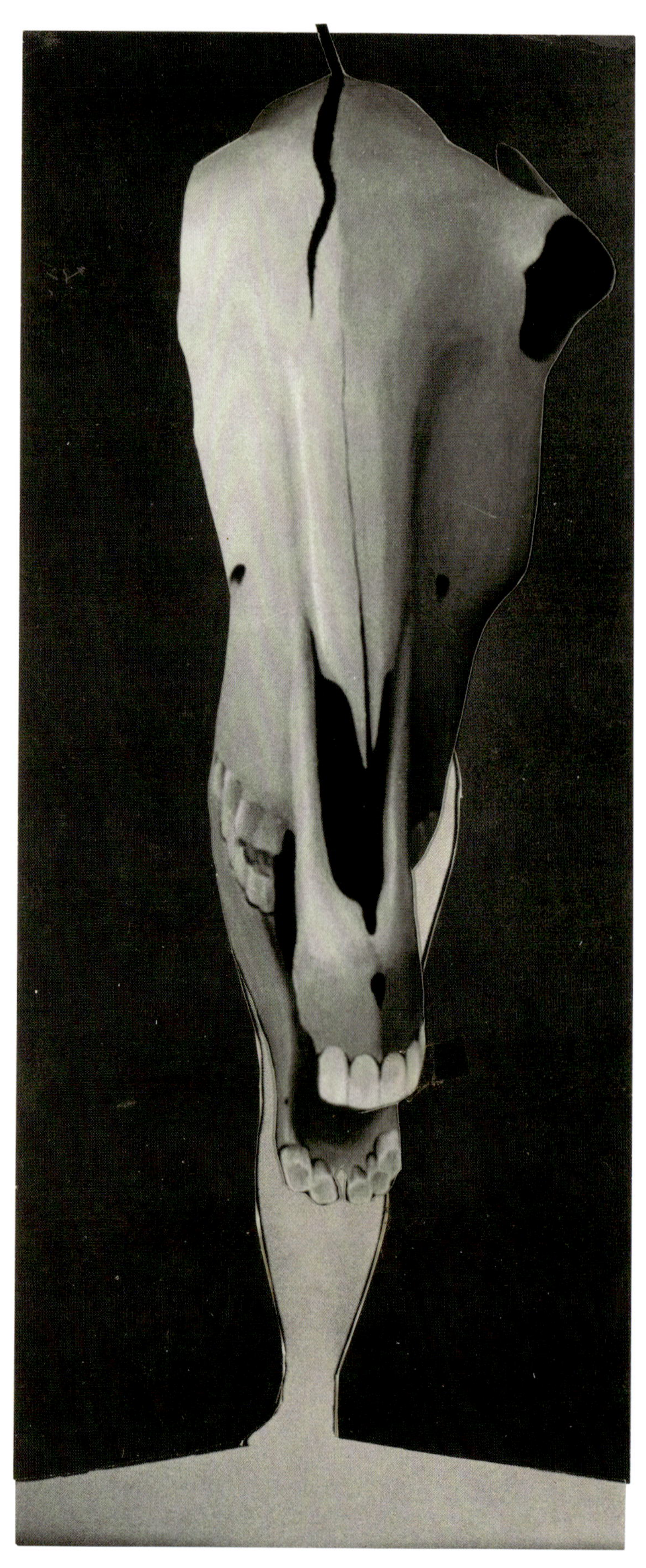

Outrageous Fortune

JAY DEFEO AND SURREALISM

MITCHELL-INNES & NASH

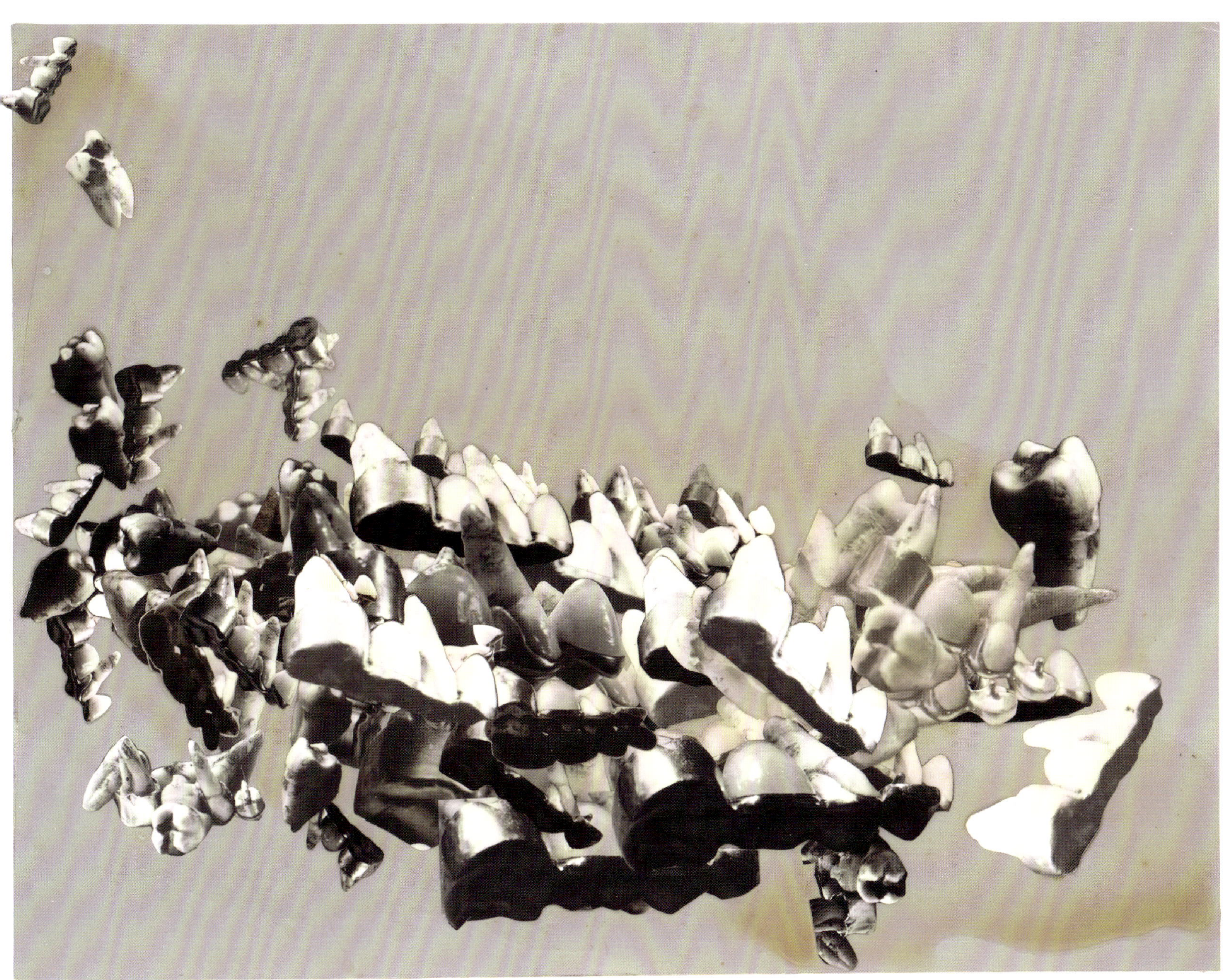

Outrageous Fortune: Jay DeFeo and Surrealism

Dana Miller

Most all of the writing on the artist Jay DeFeo (1929–1989) makes passing mention of the Surrealist quality of her work. What is considered Surrealist art today is itself so stylistically diverse and voluminous that looking for evidence of alignments with any twentieth-century artist is likely to produce positive results. And yet, this can be a worthwhile endeavor; a sustained assessment of the role this earlier movement played in DeFeo's creative output yields some unexpected results. This is not to say that DeFeo was consciously and consistently drawing on Surrealist doctrine as set out in manifestos and seminal publications, but rather that a Surrealist sensibility infuses much of her art. And specific congruencies illuminate latent aspects of her work that might otherwise seem inadvertent. Among the parallels are the incorporation of dreams and the subconscious; an interest in cameraless techniques of photography; and a fascination with the anthropomorphic machine and the fragmented body as subjects. Of the many artists associated with Surrealism, Marcel Duchamp (1887–1968) and Man Ray (1890–1976) emerge as important precursors for DeFeo. Not coincidentally both figures straddled the porous border between Dada and Surrealism and worked in a cross-disciplinary fashion. As DeFeo's career progressed in the 1970s, we know from her correspondence that she was looking at Man Ray's methods of cameraless photography and seeking what André Breton (1896–1966) termed the marvelous, or "convulsive beauty." Breton had described three types of convulsive beauty: the *érotique-voilée*,

the *explosante-fixe*, and the *magique-circonstancielle*. Looking at DeFeo's work through the filter of Breton's terminology results in surprising concurrences, intended or not.

Nearly every scholarly treatment of DeFeo's work quotes her 1959 artist's statement for the *Sixteen Americans* exhibition at the Museum of Modern Art, New York: "Only by chancing the ridiculous, can I hope for the sublime."[1] Analyses of this passage tend to focus on the lofty aspirations and gauntlet-throwing high stakes of the "ridiculous" and the "sublime." But I would argue the operative word in the statement is "chancing." That without allowing chance to affect some aspect of her process, DeFeo had no hope for achieving a sublime work. This meant not only taking risks, but also, at key moments, sharing authorship with forces of nature, randomness, or accident. This embrace of chance, or "outrageous fortune," proved to be the most significant aspect of Surrealism for DeFeo.

DeFeo emerged as a mature artist amidst the counterculture of 1950s San Francisco, a fertile milieu comparable to the Surrealists' Paris in several noteworthy ways. Her cadre of artists, poets, writers, and musicians were similarly antiestablishment,

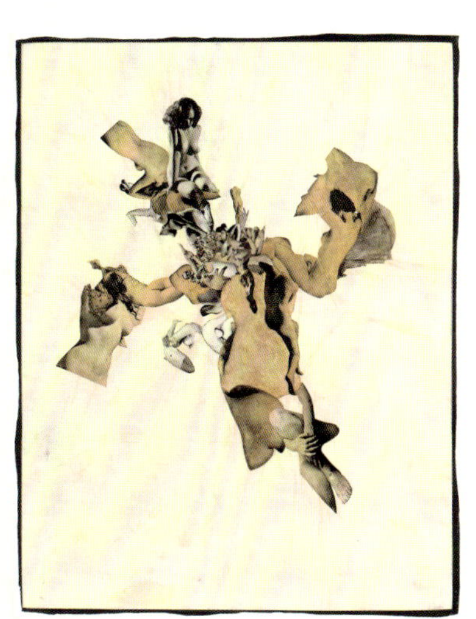
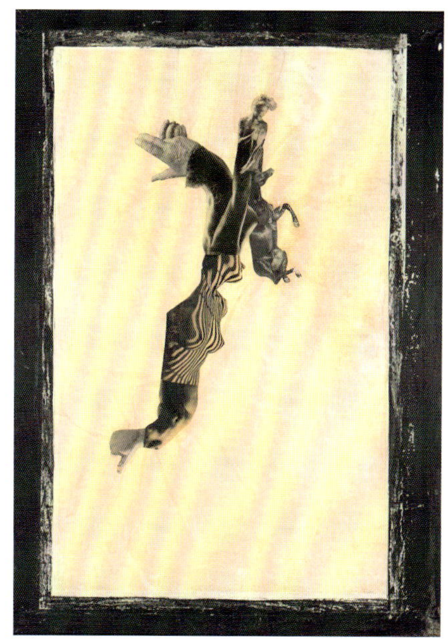

Blossom, 1958
Applaud the Black Fact, 1958

several of them having returned from serving in World War II or the Korean War disillusioned by the institutions in power. In 1957 Bruce Conner (1933–2008) and the poet Michael McClure (b. 1932) founded the Rat Bastard Protective Association, which was devoted, as Conner put it, to "people who were making things with the detritus of society, who themselves were ostracized or alienated."[2] As with the Surrealists, the literary and visual arts were intertwined within her Fillmore circle. Wally Hedrick (1928–2003), DeFeo's husband, cofounded the cooperative Six Gallery in 1954 alongside other poets and artists and it was there that Robert Duncan (1919–1988) premiered his play *Faust Foutu* and Allen Ginsberg (1926–1997) first read *Howl*. Wallace Berman (1926–1976) lived nearby for several years and his self-published poetry and art journal *Semina* was required reading during its lifespan (1955–64). Berman, DeFeo, and many of her compatriots were inspired by the work of the eighteenth-century English poet and artist William Blake (1757–1827), as were the Surrealists. In particular, Blake's belief in the existence of a truth and beauty that was beyond rational perception attracted the Surrealists who similarly viewed the perceivable world as merely symbols of other, larger truths. Not surprisingly, several of the DeFeo works that reflect Blakean ideals or iconography likewise reverberate with a Surrealist approach.

DeFeo herself often served as muse to her friends, appearing in works by Berman, Conner, and Hedrick and poems by McClure

to name just a few. And yet it is notable that she made very few portraits in the traditional sense, of herself or of others.[3] Rather, DeFeo made portrait-like depictions of objects which possessed, in her words, "some enigmatic figurative reference."[4] One notable instance is a work she titled *Landscape with Figure* (1955, cat. E2798, p. 25), which by all standard conventions would fall into the category of still life. DeFeo acknowledged that she had given it that title specifically (as opposed to its bejeweled sister work *Still Life* [c. 1955, cat. E2348, p. 27]) and that the bouquet of daisies nestled in a brandy snifter functioned as a symbolic figure.[5] The painting is an early and crucial example of the profound correlation between floral forms and the human body in DeFeo's work.

The centrifugal photomontages of both *Blossom* and *Applaud the Black Fact* (both 1958, cat. E1209, p. 7; cat. E1204, p. 7) relate to *Landscape with Figure*—that is, if you trade cut daisies for black-and-white magazine cuttings. DeFeo arranged these pinwheel pastiches primarily from excised photos of pinup girls, but also men and horses, and they are among the most formal examples of the many assemblages she made as decorations for their home, décor for parties, or sent as correspondences to friends. In a diminutive example *Untitled* (c. 1959–60, cat. E2731, p. 38), DeFeo has collaged a photograph of a friend with a guitar slung across his lap and a photo of her mouth floating above him, like a thought bubble. The typeset words "Miss Brown to You,"

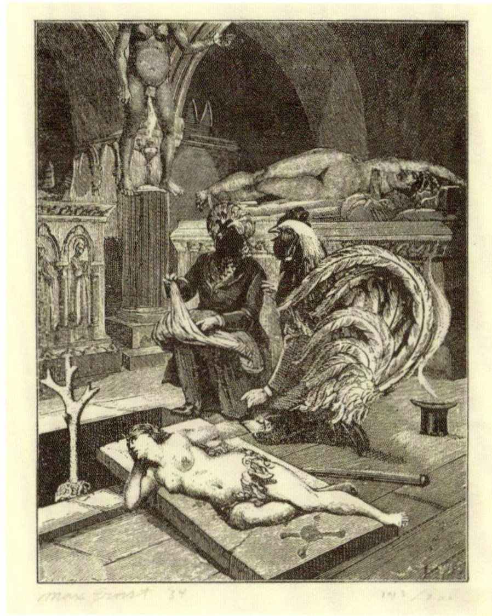

Max Ernst
From *Une Semaine de bonté*, 1934

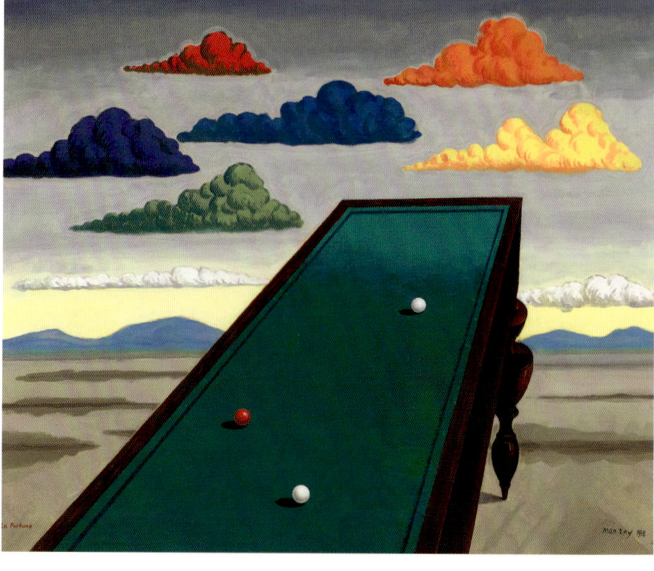

Man Ray
La Fortune, 1938

oriented so as to be legible to his downcast eyes, were taken from a Billie Holiday song. Although DeFeo considered assemblage strategies fundamental to her approach to art at that time, little of this aspect of her work remains extant.[6] As she explained, "In those days there was play time and art time for me … I did a lot of postcard art before it had, you know, a name, and a lot of little collage stuff that way. Funny kind of sort of Dada joke stuff that I just did for entertainment and relief and release and fun."[7] Her acknowledged debt to Dada collagists likely encompassed the work of Hannah Höch (1889–1978) and Max Ernst (1891–1976). Ernst's work was a source of stimulation for many of those in her circle: Berman, Conner, the artist Jess (Burgess Collins, 1923–2004), all of whom were working with a collage aesthetic, as well as the poet Philip Lamantia (1927–2005). And for several decades, possibly as early as her 1950s Fillmore period, DeFeo owned a print from *Une Semaine de bonté* (1934, p. 8), Ernst's five-part novel illustrated with nonsensical collages featuring hybrids of beast and man. Following the examples of Höch, Ernst, and others from the earlier part of the century, DeFeo took found imagery from popular culture and placed it into a new, disjunctive context with no attempt at rational narrative. *Blossom* and *Applaud the Black Fact* would have had the additional provocation of the proliferation of naked or semiclothed women. These two photomontages are perhaps the earliest instances of the fragmented female body as DeFeo's

subject—an archetypal Surrealist theme and one that reappears throughout her career.

DeFeo's playful approach to collage was aligned with the Surrealists who saw play as a means of accessing the subconscious and tapping into an unfettered and authentic mode of thinking. Most games involve some aspect of luck—whether by rolling the dice or dealing cards—and luck became a key aspect of much Dada art and then later Surrealism. Breton called this abdication of sole responsibility for the final creation *disponibilité*. Many of the Surrealists made games into works of art or artworks depicting games, such as Man Ray's iconic painting *La Fortune* (1938, p. 8). This embrace of chance factored into several strains of Surrealism including Ernst's innovation of *frottage*—a rubbing technique he developed in 1925 using the wood grain of floorboards beneath his paper to create unpremeditated drawings. DeFeo responded similarly in 1956 when she began affixing large sheets of paper to a wall in her studio for a series of tall drawings she referred to as her "grasses" period. "I had a wonderful plaster wall. I never had a wall like that since," she recalled. "And it picked up a wonderful texture with graphite on that cheap drafting paper."[8] Although there is no evidence of DeFeo knowingly imitating Ernst in this particular respect, these works demonstrate a shared sensitivity to the textures of their environment. The "grasses" were also an early indication

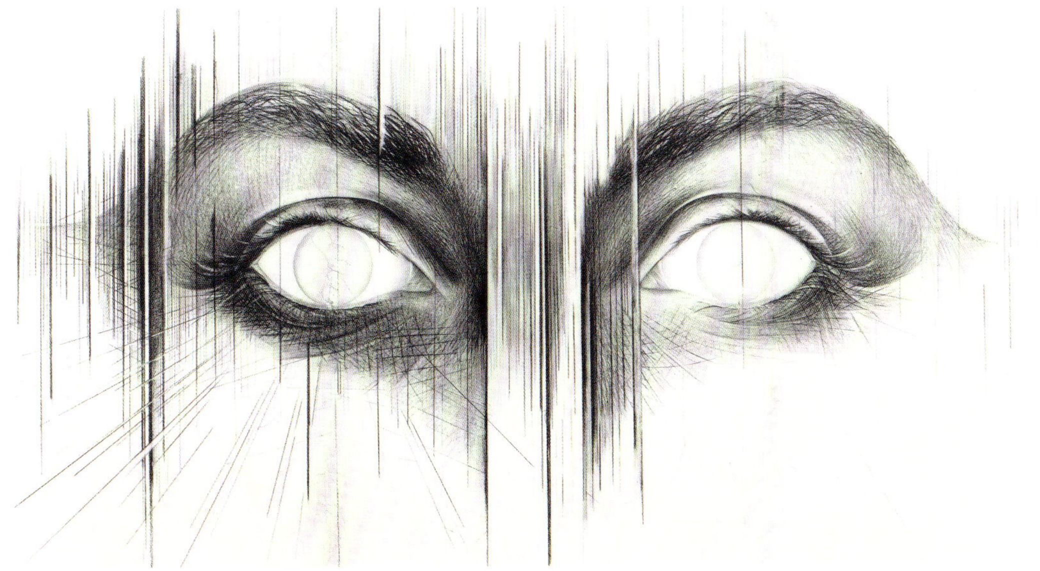

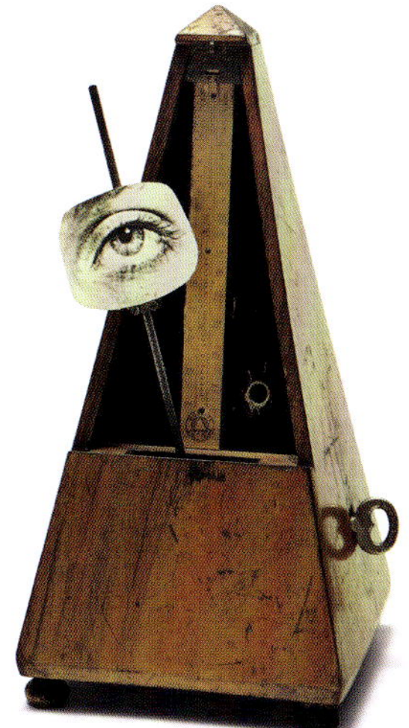

The Eyes, 1958

Man Ray
_Indestructible Object (or Object to Be
Destroyed)_, 1964

that DeFeo, like Ernst, was willing to accommodate outside forces into her compositional process.

Following the "grasses" drawings DeFeo made a seven-foot-wide drawing based on a tiny cropped photo of her own eyes. _The Eyes_ (1958, cat. E1212, p. 9) is the closest she ever got to a mimetic self-portrait. More than once DeFeo described the drawing as having suffered "The Slings and Arrows of Outrageous Fortune," quoting Shakespeare's famous soliloquy from _Hamlet_.[9] The first assault occurred shortly after its completion when an attempt at mounting failed and the paper tore right through the center of one of the irises. DeFeo was philosophical about the damage _The Eyes_ withstood, because, as she explained: "Even though I have very defined and meticulous areas in my work, I oftentimes use the accidental occurrence as part of the image."[10] DeFeo compared the tears in _The Eyes_ to the extensive cracks in Duchamp's magnum opus _The Bride Stripped Bare by Her Bachelors, Even (The Large Glass)_ (1915–23, p. 10), which occurred in 1927, and which Duchamp thereby accepted as part of the work. As DeFeo explained, "the cracks kind of became part of the composition. And I have a kind of a feeling that they sort of needed to be part of the piece, like the crack in Duchamp's _Glass_ so to speak."[11] The notion of _The Eyes_ suffering at the hands of Fortune is particularly ironic given that the goddess Fortuna of classical mythology is usually depicted as being blind.

DeFeo said she needed to make _The Eyes_ in order to envision the works that were to follow, most especially _The Rose_ (1958–66, cat. E1000, p. 10), which she worked on for almost eight years. DeFeo refused to sell _The Eyes_ and it hung for some period of time in her studio, acting as a companion and witness, not dissimilar to the function of Man Ray's _Object to Be Destroyed_ (1923). When making the earliest version of this adjusted readymade, Man Ray attached a photograph of an eye to the hand of a metronome. The eye ticked back and forth in the studio, providing a soothing presence and an audience. Man Ray remade the sculpture in 1964, after it was destroyed, titling that iteration _Indestructible Object_ (p. 9), and then remade it again in an edition in 1971 with the title _Perpetual Motif_. Having undergone several rounds of damage and conservation in the decades since the first tear, _The Eyes_ now resides in the collection of the Whitney Museum of American Art, New York—DeFeo's own indestructible object.

Like _The Eyes_, Duchamp's _Large Glass_ was a stimulus and solace for DeFeo during the long gestation of _The Rose_. As she explained in a 1961 letter: "We have a tape of some remarks made by Duchamp—Answering them 'yes I worked on the large glass twelve years. Yes, I suppose I am a meticulous man.' Well, those words comfort me. I, too, am meticulous. But let's hope it isn't twelve years! Nevertheless—if it is—or more—so what?"[12] DeFeo had become well versed in Duchamp's legacy

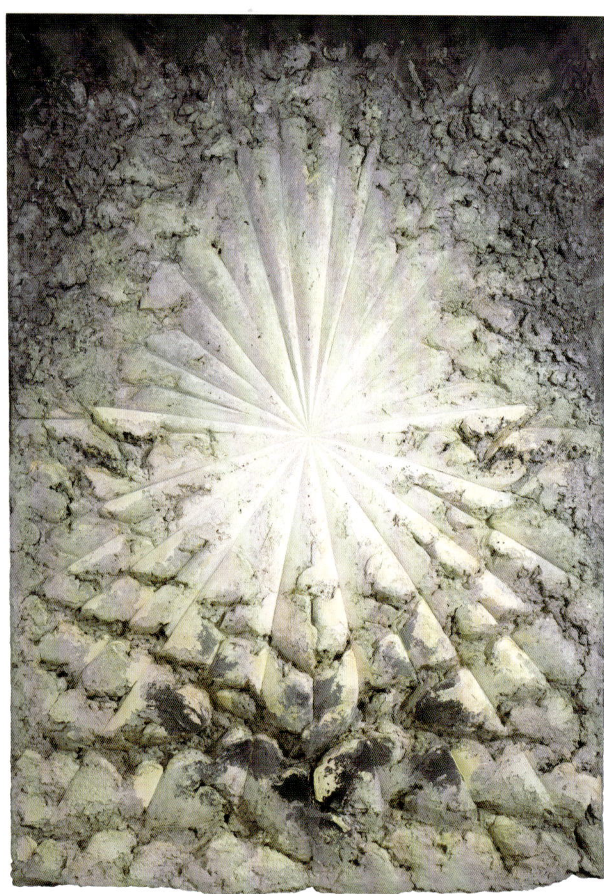

The Rose, 1958–66

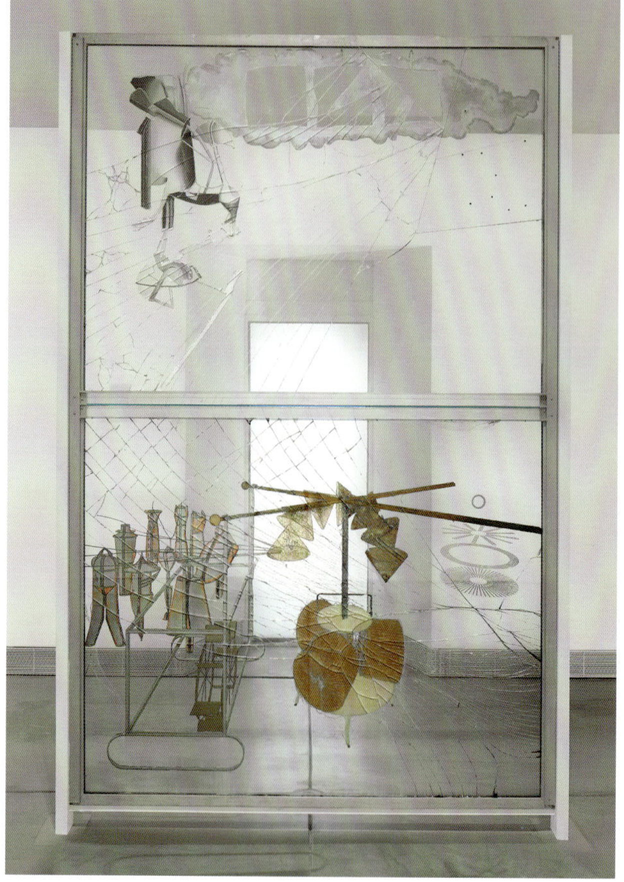

Marcel Duchamp
The Bride Stripped Bare by Her Bachelors, Even (The Large Glass), 1915–23

after marrying Hedrick. As she explained: "As soon as I met Wally, he [Duchamp] became very familiar. Because he was one of Wally's greatest gods, always. And actually, having met Wally and finding out something, I found that there was a bit of latent material there for me."[13] DeFeo's identification with Duchamp only intensified after she followed *The Rose* to the Pasadena Art Museum in 1966. Her close friend, the curator Walter Hopps, had organized a Duchamp retrospective there in 1963 and DeFeo recalled that even three years later, for her personally, "the impact of Duchamp was very felt. Very, very felt."[14]

In addition to finding parallels between the development of *The Rose* and *The Large Glass*, DeFeo found connections with Duchamp's alternate persona, Rrose Sélavy. In the 1970s DeFeo took to signing her correspondence to Conner "Rose," or sometimes just "R." Duchamp chose the name Rrose Sélavy because its French pronunciation is understood as *Eros, c'est la*

vie, which translates to "Sex, that's life." Perhaps for DeFeo, who used just one "r" for her "Rose Selavy" persona, the adjusted translation would be *Rose, c'est la vie*, or "Rose, that's life." It would not be unfair to say that for much of her career the fate of *The Rose* was inextricably linked to her general welfare. Florine Stettheimer (1871–1944), the American artist and friend of Duchamp, similarly used flowers symbolically, most notably as stand-ins for self-portraits. DeFeo did not learn about the cloistered Stettheimer until 1975 but was immediately fascinated by her. Shortly thereafter she wrote in her journal about a painting in progress: "reminding me of Florine S. [Stettheimer] again. She, too, preoccupied with Rose Selavy (my own persona—at least occasionally)."[15] DeFeo's close association between floral forms and the female body, established in *Landscape with Figure*, extended to her own self-identification. *La Vie en Rose* with a twist.

After completing *The Rose* and taking a roughly four-year
hiatus DeFeo began to regain her artistic footing again in 1970.
Some of her earliest works from this period reference *The Eyes*
explicitly, such as *Untitled* (1970, cat. E2351, p. 79), *Untitled*
(c. 1972, cat. E3295, p. 92), or implicitly with works such as
Merz's Eye (1971) and *After Image* (1970). Vision, in all of its
many connotations had become a preoccupation for DeFeo—
her "perpetual motif." She was also retraining her eye to see
through the lens of a camera. Much in the same way Breton
and his fellow Surrealists prowled the streets and flea markets
of Paris on the lookout for objects that exerted a magnetic pull,
DeFeo took photographs of shop windows in Larkspur, her new
hometown. It was an exercise in Surrealist looking, conscious or
not, and she naturally gravitated to those objects that suggested
a veiled corporeal form, that same "enigmatic figurative
reference." Many of these images recall the photography of
Eugène Atget (1857–1927), whose haunting pictures of Paris
storefronts were co-opted by the Surrealists to advance their
arguments. Among DeFeo's figurative non-figures is the black
and white outfit hanging limply without a mannequin or body to
fill its contours in *Untitled* (1972, cat. P0102, p. 54). The uncanny
silhouette summons her *Landscape with Figure* and *Still Life*. The
floral fabric "head" atop of which she attached beads and floral
embroideries in the latter has transmogrified into a lace blouse.

In her early years of experimenting with the camera, DeFeo
photographed several remnants of prior work, resuscitating
past creative efforts as a way of forging ahead. This allowed her
to dive midstream into her often cyclical process of working,
rather than having to begin afresh. In 1973 she mounted the
central fragment of an unfinished drawing from 1958, titled it
White Spica (1958/73), and shot it repeatedly (both 1973, cat.
P0784J, p. 101; cat. P1527, p. 102). Spica is a star in the Virgo
constellation and the radial symmetry and careful delineation
of angles and vectors in the drawing bring to mind the compass
roses used for navigation. *White Spica* might have served, literally

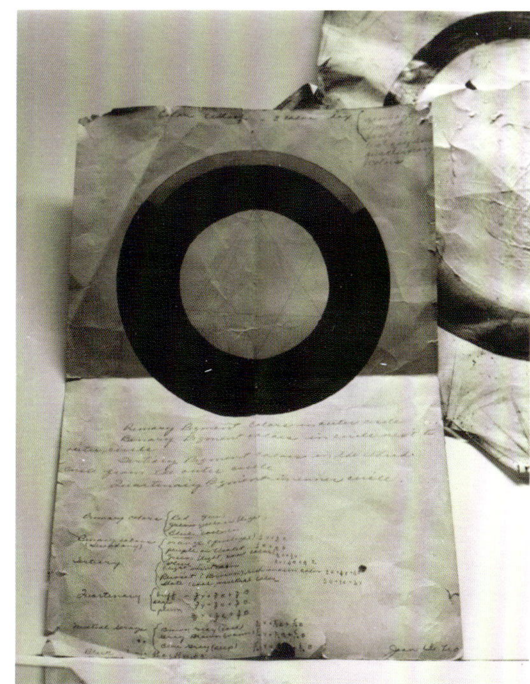

Untitled, 1973

and figuratively, as a guide for DeFeo as she regained her
bearings, much the way stars and compass roses guide sailors at
sea. In several of her *White Spica* images DeFeo played with one
of Man Ray's favorite photographic techniques, solarization,
accomplished by exposing the photographic positive to light
while developing. The solarized fragment in *Untitled (White
Spica)* takes on an almost silvery halo effect while obscuring the
distinction between figure and ground. Compositionally, *White
Spica* harkens back further to a color wheel exercise DeFeo
completed in high school, one in which the circumscription
of triangles continued to resonate long afterward. DeFeo
photographed the two objects side by side in works such as
Untitled (1973, P0333E, p. 11), making their direct connection
explicit. Next to the color wheel *White Spica* calls to mind
other DeFeo works with a rotational dynamism including the
pinwheel photomontages of the 1950s, photographs she took in
1973 of electrical fans, and later drawings of a tape dispenser.
It also evokes various wheel allegories, among them, the wheel
of fortune.

In addition to capturing the remains of older work, DeFeo
photographed fragments of her own body. She suffered from
periodontal disease and the teeth she had extracted, along with

the bridge created from a combination of her teeth and false teeth, appear repeatedly in her works from the early 1970s. The most significant works in the series are the black and white pendant paintings *Crescent Bridge I* and *Crescent Bridge II* (1970–72), seen in photographs of her studio from this time (1971, cat. P1607, p. 96; 1971, cat. P1012D, p. 97; 1973, cat. P1020C, p. 93). DeFeo's extracted teeth were the physical substantiation of what Shakespeare's Hamlet described as "The heartache, and the thousand natural shocks / That flesh is heir to." DeFeo treats them gingerly, like relics or pearls in photos such as *Untitled* (1973, cat. P0990E, p. 106), in which she nestled them inside a clamshell. One of the most unusual works to come of her dental bridge is *Traveling Portrait (Chance Landscape)* (1973, cat. E2352, p. 5). She explained its origins as follows: "I had about a million photographs of that bridge … this was a chance operation. I didn't know what the hell to do with them. So, I just put a whole bunch of acrylic media on this board and I just let them drift at random, after spending heaven knows how many hours and hours and hours cutting these things out."[16] The teeth slid downward toward the bottom of the paperboard, like a rock slide settling into its angle of repose. The jumbled outcroppings of teeth and the infinite expanse of gray at the top of the resulting work are reminiscent of Yves Tanguy's (1900–1950) dystopian panoramas. And so what likely was conceived initially as a symbolic portrait was rendered a Surrealist landscape.[17] DeFeo referred to this work as "a chance operation," rather than a "chance incident" or "accident," which implies some intentionality on her part—an experiment in courting chance.

The melancholy painting *Trap* (1972, cat. E1321, p. *77*) is perhaps the most providential example of chance intervening in DeFeo's work. A moth remains ensnared at the spot along the painting's ovoid contour where it landed on the surface and was unable to free itself.[18] Rather than being the fly in the ointment, DeFeo saw it as a fortuitous occurrence. She wrote that it was "a 'chance happening' in the process of the work, around which

I based the meaning of the piece."[19] She may or may not have known that Pablo Picasso (1881–1973) composed *Composition au Papillon* (1932) with a butterfly adhered to the canvas or that Jackson Pollock (1912–1956) allowed a trapped cockroach to remain in his majestic painting *No. 1, 1950 (Lavender Mist)* (1950). *Trap* exemplifies one of Breton's aspects of convulsive beauty, namely the *explosante-fixe* or the "expiration of movement."[20] The moth has been permanently arrested or "fixed" by the painting, and although the painting may have been intended as a portrait or landscape, its final result is nothing if not an affecting still life.

Lured to DeFeo's painting like an insect to a flower, the moth's presence imparts *Trap* with an unmistakable air of sorrow and layers of significance. DeFeo might very well have known that Duchamp, the master of the punning title, created a readymade called *Trébuchet (Trap)* (1917/64, p. 13), which consisted of a coatrack nailed to the floor of his New York studio. An avid chess player, Duchamp was himself referencing a chess move used to trick the opposition. With this precedent in mind, could we reconsider DeFeo's painting as the bait and we the viewer are the ones trapped, transfixed by the pitiful casualty? Or, could the painting be read as a metaphor for the artistic struggle and it is the artist who is trapped in her work?

DeFeo gravitated toward subjects that conveyed the vulnerability of the body and her antennae were highly attuned to objects bearing wounds or signs of age. Worn and mottled surfaces had fascinated DeFeo as far back as her European sojourn in the early 1950s.[21] She photographed gnarled driftwood (1972, cat. P0309, p. 51), the mangled metal of a wrecked car (1973, cat. P1568B, p. 42), the carcasses of burnt tortillas (1972, cat. P0988, p. 82), her tinfoil-covered bathroom (1973, cat. P0502, p. 61), and the petals of a rose (1973, cat. P0408C, p. 100). The crushed and layered paint from the vestiges of *The Estocada* (abandoned in 1965) appears in numerous photographs from the early 1970s, alone and paired with other highly textured surfaces. But

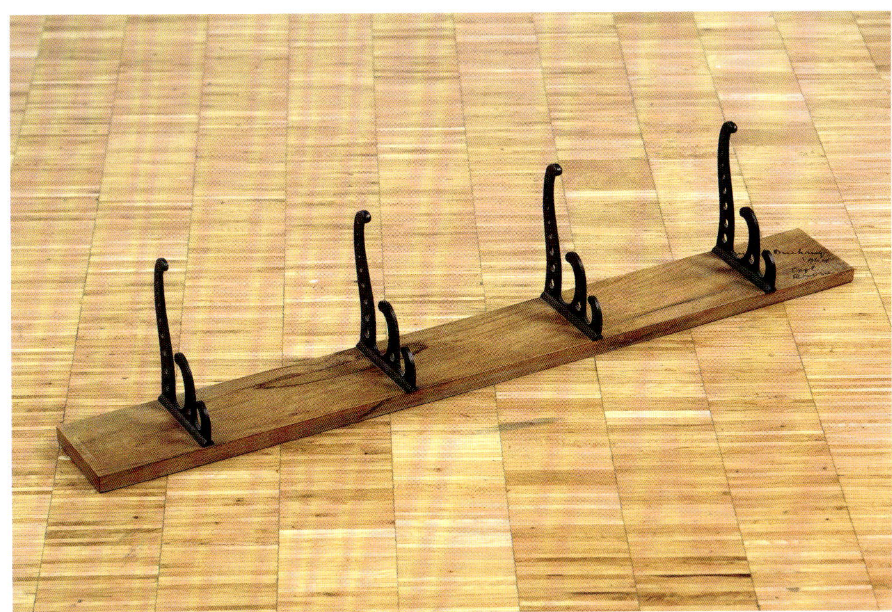

Marcel Duchamp
Trébuchet (Trap), 1917/64

among the more enigmatic items DeFeo photographed was the tattered orthopedic cast that her dog wore after it had been hit by a car (1973, cat. P1803, pp. 62–63). The wrapped bandages, suspended from a pin by a frayed cord, exemplified the broken and dilapidated objects she so esteemed, more evidence of "the thousand natural shocks / That flesh is heir to." Of course it was not lost on DeFeo that the dog's cast bore the semblance of a leg without an actual corporeal presence. DeFeo would depict bodily effigies repeatedly, including water goggles, shoe trees, and a single, worn high heel shoe (both 1973, cat. P0605A, p. 104; cat. P0607A, p. 105). The shoe evokes both the dog's discarded cast and the abandoned slipper of Cinderella stories.[22] DeFeo also recognized the linguistic complexities presented by the cast which had belonged to her dog R. Mutt. DeFeo named the dog for the signature Duchamp inscribed upon his most famous readymade, the porcelain urinal he turned upside down and titled *Fountain* (1917). Naming a mixed-breed puppy R. Mutt is an inside joke to begin with, especially considering that Duchamp was the artist most adept at punning. The cast was a readymade in the tradition of *Fountain*, and at the same time a sculpture molded for the dog's leg. In the latter sense it recalls DeFeo's youthful experiments with plaster sculpture in the early 1950s, when, one should note, she named her two kittens Plaster and Rags.

Like R. Mutt's cast, DeFeo photographed busts and mannequins as a way to approach figuration without a trace of portraiture. Mannequins were a mainstay of Surrealist art, appearing in works and installations by Giorgio de Chirico (1888–1978), Salvador Dalí (1904–1989), Duchamp, André Masson (1896–1987), and Man Ray, to name just a few. Breton's 1924 *First Manifesto of Surrealism* put forth the mannequin as the quintessential modern object for inciting the marvelous. It wasn't simply DeFeo's adoption of mannequins that linked her to Surrealism but rather the disquieting manner in which she employed them. A photo taken during one of the classes she was teaching at the San Francisco Museum of Art, *Untitled* (1975, cat. P1479E, p. 49) features a model reclining with her hand atop an armless mannequin's bald head, the body and its uncanny double side by side. In other photographs a pair of dislocated mannequin legs are clad in stockings tattered with runs and tears suggesting the morning after a hard night, or more ominously, a body under threat. A particularly unsettling photo collage (1974, cat. E2334, p. 53) finds the legs sited between a set of train tracks. The image brings to mind the re-articulated limbs of Hans Bellmer's (1902–1975) dolls as well as the gendered cinema trope of a woman tied up and left by a villain on a set of railroad tracks. With these works DeFeo returns to the dislocated bodies of her 1950s collages while tapping into the dark eroticism and implied violence that underlie a great deal of Surrealist art.

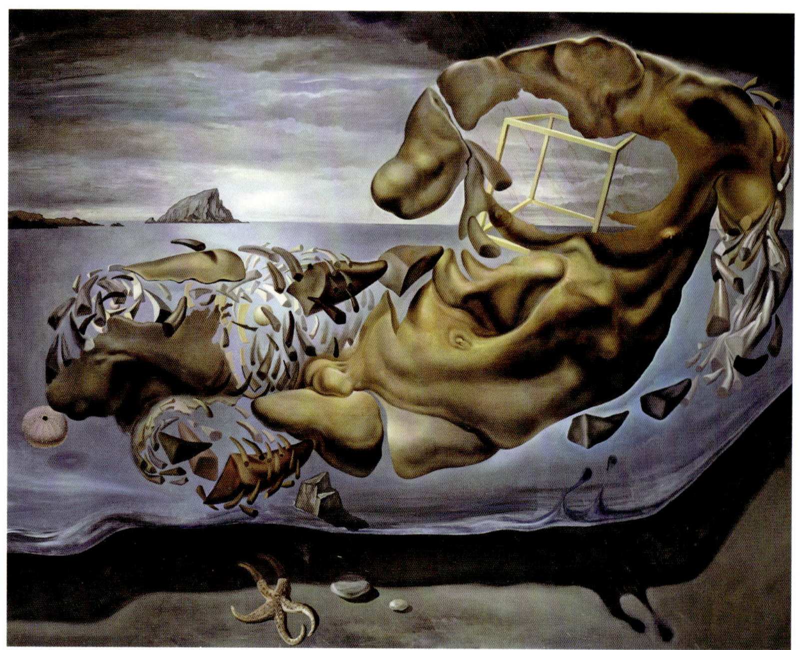

Salvador Dalí
Creazione dell'uomo (Creation of
Man), *Rhinocerontic Figure of Illisus
of Phidias*, c. 1954

The mid-1970s marked a period of intense collage work for DeFeo and in many ways these works are the preeminent synthesis of the destruct/construct dialectic that drives much of her production. In 1973 Conner had suggested that she take pictures of the "things [around her] and turn them into other stuff … collage things."[23] DeFeo and Conner had such sustained phone conversations that DeFeo took to calling him "Telephone" and she began signing her correspondences to him "Rose." Among the items that DeFeo focused her lens upon was an old candlestick style telephone, which she altered by adding a flame light bulb into the receiver holder as seen in *Untitled* (1973, cat. P0453A, p. 43), a thematic association she likely appreciated. A Eureka vacuum cleaner (1973–74, cat. E1327, p. 68; 1974, cat. E1734, p. 69), a golf bag, and her camera tripod (1973, cat. E3292, p. 41) also have recurring roles and DeFeo combines these inanimate objects into hybrid mechanistic creatures (interestingly ones that mimic the mechanics of speaking or breathing). They bring to mind the "mechanomorphology" of Duchamp's coffee mill, chocolate grinder, and other apparatus from *The Large Glass*, as well as the photomontages Ernst made from repurposed scientific publications. DeFeo's idiosyncratic juxtapositions fulfill the famous Surrealist adage attributed to the nineteenth-century poet Isidore Ducasse (1846–1870) of beauty as "the chance meeting on a dissecting table of a sewing machine and an umbrella."[24] Indeed DeFeo acknowledged in her journal that the "law of chance seems to guide me in these little collages."[25] It's most likely that DeFeo knew of Ducasse's mantra when she took a photograph of a mysterious plastic-covered object bound with rope, *Untitled* (1974, cat. P0517B, p. 57). The similarities are strong enough to assume that DeFeo's photo is a winking nod to the Man Ray photograph, purportedly of a wrapped sewing machine, entitled *The Enigma of Isidore Ducasse* (1920).

On May 11, 1973, DeFeo made a series of photographs that she titled *Salvador Dalí's Birthday Party* (it was indeed his 69th birthday). She manipulated her photographic chemicals and paper directly, responding to the fluids in hand as they responded to her movements. Of all her works the chemigrams are the closest to the Surrealist pillar of "pure psychic automatism," the relinquishing of rational control and premeditation.[26] As such, these photographs are among DeFeo's most abstract works. And yet the same symbol shapes that are found in her earlier works often emerged from these tactile explorations, as if lodged in a subconscious alphabet that would inevitably find expression in her work. The soft contours of DeFeo's runs and spills, fixed onto the paper, evoke the liquefaction of Dalí's invented universe. And just as Dalí's imagery bent the rules of the physical world in paintings such as *Creazione dell'uomo* (Creation of Man), *Rhinocerontic Figure of Illisus of Phidias* (c. 1954, p. 14), DeFeo bent the rules of photography by eliminating both model and camera. It's hard to imagine a better descriptor for DeFeo's birthday photographs than the one that Dalí routinely used to refer to his paintings: "hand-painted dream photographs." Her dreamy photos are lyrical rather than labored, even when traces of her hand are visible as in *Untitled (Salvador Dalí's Birthday Party)* (1973, cat. P0542, p. 109).

DeFeo made other chemigrams that year, several of which take her handprint as their subject. The ghostly *Untitled* (1973, cat. P0540, p. 103) seems to be emitting heat and light from the darkness, like a reverse shadow. The photograph is simultaneously an image, a signature, and a document of its making—an emphatic assertion of its handmade nature. DeFeo experimented with other cameraless photographic processes, including photograms, the technique Man Ray explored extensively in the early part of the twentieth century and which he called "Rayography." The "Rayograms" bestowed everyday items with halos and transparent layers, revealing hidden qualities imperceptible to the naked eye. In the summer of 1974 DeFeo saw the exhibition *Man Ray: Photo Graphics* at the San Francisco Museum of Art and wrote in a letter shortly thereafter: "The Man Ray show inspired me to be more comfortable with my approach. I have neither the temperament—nor the facilities— for a hard-core technical path to perfection."[27] It was about this time that DeFeo added the photocopy machine to her toolset, extending her photographic exploration beyond the darkroom. The ability to compose and print images almost instantaneously suited her "temperament" well. DeFeo used some of these photocopies, alongside her chemigrams and photograms, for collages, in part as a solution for "what to do with bad prints."[28] The poignant collage she made of her mother's aged hand uses a shadowy chemigram as a ground, so that the "enigmatic figural reference" emerges dramatically from a deep, indefinite space

(1973, cat. E2328, p. 52). The camera picked up on every line and crevice of skin, much as it did with her handprint image, reveling in the highly textural landscapes of the human body.

By the mid-1970s DeFeo had also started reading Carl Jung (1875–1961), and keeping a dream journal. In May of 1975 she mentions reading a passage from the book *Abstraction in Art and Nature* by Nathan Cabot Hale (b. 1925) to her therapist.[29] Although we don't know the precise passage she read, it was within a section entitled "Light and Darkness, Black and White," and the following is a possible candidate that nonetheless captures the psychological tone of the writing: "There is an inner light and darkness that is visible in our brains for we can picture things that we do not see when our eyes are closed. We create inner visions and dreams out of this inner light and darkness. We literally draw pictures with our mind."[30]

That fall the first mention of Breton appears in her journal. And so while it is likely that Breton's ideas infiltrated her thinking long before, we can say definitively that DeFeo was drawing upon the Surrealist's writings by late 1975. At that time Conner was also experimenting with cameraless photography and DeFeo began using an announcement for Conner's show of photograms as a substrate and stimulant. The one-page announcement featured two reproductions of Conner's life-size photograms of his body, which he called "angels." The angels appear as hourglass silhouettes demarcated by the darkness that surrounds them, with Conner's handprints at the forefront. They are decidedly feminine and statuesque, like marble caryatids, and for DeFeo they possessed Breton's "convulsive beauty."[31] DeFeo combined these invitations with photographs and other photocopies in collages with images of the flame light bulb, vacuum, flowers, candlestick telephone, and photographs of friends' paintings (1975–76, cat. E2943, p. 46; 1975–76, cat. E2941, p. 47; 1976, cat. E2933, p. 2). She referred to them in her journal as her "paper dolls" silhouettes."[32] Conner had sent her

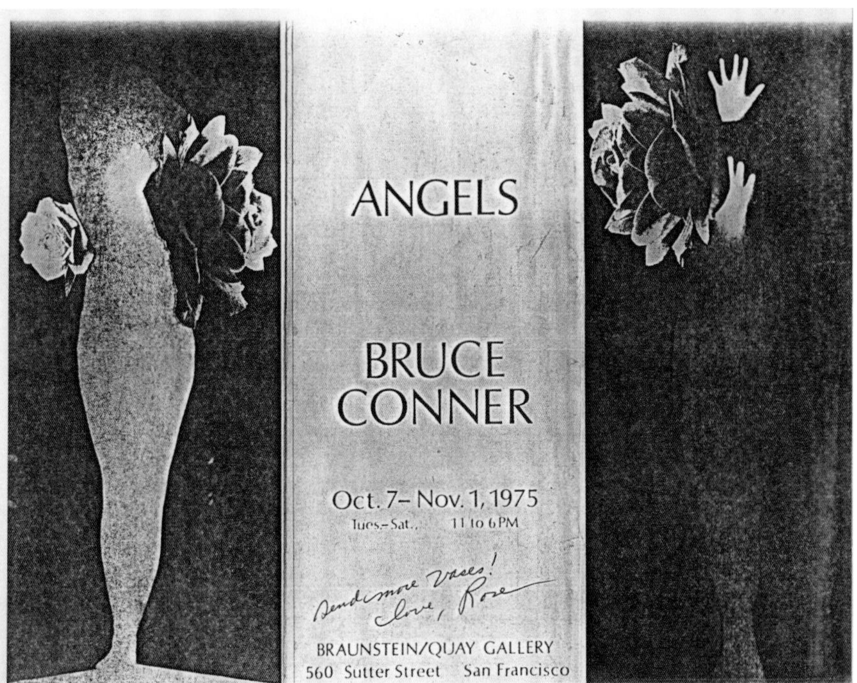

Inscribed photocopy of
Untitled, 1975

a stack of the invitations to use after DeFeo wrote to him on a photocopy of the invite requesting extras. She had collaged roses atop the figures and inscribed it, "Send more vases!" As if to underscore this particular use of floral arrangements as a metaphor for the human form, DeFeo signed the missive "Rose," her "sometimes persona."

DeFeo consistently gravitated toward certain shapes and forms throughout her career, making it difficult to determine where one thematic grouping ends and another begins. She considered a series of bone images she began in 1975 as related to her Conner announcement or "angels" series.[33] DeFeo had become mesmerized by the strange and uncanny look of a lamb bone in her kitchen pot. After her dog Merz absconded with the bone, she went to the butcher the following week with a drawing she had made of the bone, hoping to locate a similar cut of lamb as a replacement. DeFeo also saw affinities between the contours of the bone images and her favorite candlestick telephone, likely the ball joint that was "so similar in form" to the circular mouthpiece.[34] She chose to combine those two objects in several collages (1975, cat. E2060, p. 70; 1976, cat. E3275, p. 71), creating an unlikely web of relationships between Conner's angels, bones, and telephones.

Of all her works, the photographs, drawings, and collages she made of her tripod and what she called "its dress" most exemplify the incorporation of accident into her work. DeFeo referred to the origin story of how the tripod came to be "dressed," as a "chance incident."[35] She had been working on a drawing and one evening a drunken friend came over uninvited and vomited on the paper. DeFeo anxiously washed the drawing as best as she could and draped it over the tripod to dry. This new configuration so struck her that she left the drawing atop the tripod and proceeded to photograph and draw the arrangement. As she explained, the whole event was serendipitous as the abject intervention of another had benefitted the work. "I liked it a lot better now that somebody had violated it besides myself."[36] Secondarily, the anthropomorphic tripod onto which DeFeo had previously projected male attributes, gained its own alternate female persona, much to her delight.

Not surprisingly, DeFeo chose not to preserve some accidents or missteps and she kept a collection of hundreds of used erasers in her studio, remainders and reminders of her intensive drawing efforts. She stretched and kneaded the worn erasers into sculptural forms that she used as models for photographs. The erasers also provided a specific and highly sculptural model to work from—one that would defy easy attribution. DeFeo's eraser photographs are reminiscent of Brassaï's (1899–1984) involuntary sculptures or *sculptures involontaires* (1979, cat. E3026, p. 17), images he took of old bus tickets, a kneaded piece of bread, and other objects sculpted by a distracted and unpremeditated hand. Like Brassaï's objects, DeFeo's erasers were partially decomposed castoffs and readymades at the same time. The hand-worn look born of repeated use that distinguishes these objects in photographs is veiled in DeFeo's drawings and paintings of the same subject, so much so that *Untitled* (*Eraser* series) (1979, cat. E1895, p. 74) resembles organic matter, perhaps a bone fragment or the cartilage structure of a wing.

In a few rare instances DeFeo used existing works of sculpture as models, as with the Roman copy of a bronze statue of a Maenad by the ancient Greek sculptor Skopas (c. 360 BCE) she found in a library book.[37] Having long ago lost its upper limbs and much of its lower limbs, the sculpture possesses a sense of archeological time but also mimics the fragmented bodies of her 1950s collages. Its deteriorated and decomposed surface likely only enhanced its beauty for DeFeo. She paired the photocopy repeatedly with her collection of drawing compasses in images from 1979 (cat. E2989, p. 90; cat. E2990, p. 91; cat. E2994, p. 90), and in other variations they are joined by additional symbolically charged objects such as bones and nail clippers. Juxtapositions of metal and stone, linear and curvilinear, human and mechanistic reverberate between the superimposed layers of reproduction in a way that Isidore Ducasse would have approved. DeFeo had arranged the chance meeting on a photocopier bed of an ancient sculpture and drawing instrument.

Throughout the 1970s DeFeo continued to paint using acrylics, often pairing them with charcoal on paper. DeFeo slowly reintroduced oil paint into her palette in the early 1980s though she still often worked on paper and with a combination of media.

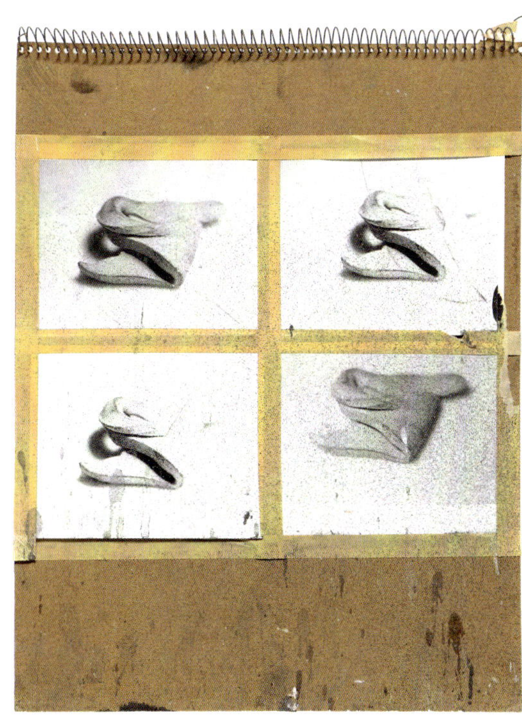

Untitled, 1979

The drill bit or screw-like form in *Chiaro* (1985, cat. E1037, p. 29), along with its sibling *Scuro* (1985), signals earlier works with centrifugal compositions or rotational dynamics. These include her photographs of electric fans or *Collage for Bruce Conner* (1975), in which she attached the rotary portion of her telephone to an "angel" cutout. These oil paintings also continue her query from the decade before into the aesthetic possibilities of utilitarian objects and tools. She frequently returned to a strong central image in her paintings from the 1980s—an "enigmatic figurative reference"—veiling her precise subject with painterly effects. DeFeo once said that she preferred that viewers not identify the subjects of her paintings. Once they do so, "they lose sight of what I'm attempting to do; that is, portray the esthetic harmony resulting from the uniting of the geometric and organic forms."[38] But her imagery is ambiguous primarily because her subjects weren't objects from the real world, rather they were a combination of items synthesized or collaged in her imagination. Not surprisingly, DeFeo often struggled to fix them in her paintings. "These fleeting images truly are like dreams," she wrote. "Nailing it down seems to remove the magic. & one can only hope to discover another in ptg—(while trying to 'nail down' something else.) It's a slippery fish."[39]

Throughout her career DeFeo conceived of her works in relation to one another and often made works in pairs or groupings, sometimes spanning decades. *Bride* (cat. E1040, pp. 34–35), her 1986 oil painting was apparently the bride of *Doctor Jazz*, an oil painting she made twenty-eight years prior.[40] *Doctor Jazz* is unique in that it is among the very few paintings of DeFeo's that might allude to the male body, one of the few available "bachelors" in her oeuvre. Its vertical format is almost entirely encompassed by an upright, highly phallic form, though it is also reminiscent of a pistil, the female anatomy of a flower. The parenthetical description of *Untitled (Reclining Figure)* (1986, cat. E1314, pp. 36–37), a work related to *Bride*, indicates that an axial shift has taken place and the female figure is now in repose. Given DeFeo's attachment to Duchamp, one cannot escape comparing her *Bride* to his paintings *Bride* (1912), *The Passage from Virgin to Bride* (1912), and *The Bride Stripped Bare by Her Bachelors, Even (The Large Glass)*. The graceful, curved shapes may summon details from Duchamp's two oil paintings, but they are in fact modeled in part after an ornately carved chair DeFeo kept in her studio. As before, DeFeo chose not to use a human figure as a model, but rather an object designed to accommodate the body. The spiral at the left of the painting, more apparent in several studies for the work (both 1986, cat. E2713, p. 73; 1986, cat. E2714, p. 75), is partially derived from the elaborate armrest but reprises a form found in DeFeo's works going back as far as the red f-hole graphic in her "Miss Brown to You" collage (*Untitled*, c. 1959–60, cat. E2731, p. 38). Although dating from more than a decade prior, DeFeo's photographs of a violin from 1971 (cat. P0382, p. 19) seem to offer clues to *Bride* and the brown-tinted *Untitled (Reclining Figure)*. The violin is pictured prone, accentuating the scroll, while the unbound hair of the bow drapes loosely over the neck. Of course the violin was used as a visual metaphor for the female body most famously by Man Ray in *Le Violon d'Ingres* (1924), the image of the back of a seated woman upon which he inscribed two f-holes. There's no documentary evidence that DeFeo was looking at her violin images while painting these works but the cyclical way in which she worked validates such associations. As she explained, "I maintain a kind of consciousness of everything I've ever done while I'm engaged on a current work."[41] The spiral that recurs in DeFeo's work applies as well to the chronology of her career as she returns to certain themes and preoccupations again and again. The haunting nature of much of her work is due in great part to the echoes of her former works.

Rather than succumb to the slings and arrows sent her way, DeFeo utilized chance, accident, and "outrageous fortune" as tools in her creative arsenal. She embraced chance in her process and frequently considered herself lucky when accident intervened in her work. At times she recognized the specifically *outrageous* nature of fortune—its capacity for cruelty, irony, munificence, and synchronicity. Works that DeFeo intended as portraits became still lifes or landscapes, or vice versa. In other instances, fortune's dealings infused her work with the frailty of the human condition. The Surrealists viewed life as a succession of unpredictable shocks, the only response to which was to welcome the irrational, unexplainable, and the absurd. In this way they, particularly Duchamp and Man Ray, provided a model for chancing the ridiculous. DeFeo took enormous chances throughout her career by changing media, shifting styles, and deviating beyond the usual bounds of scale, efficiency, practicality, or propriety. Without this risk-taking, this faith in both herself and forces larger than herself, DeFeo would not have made works of such raw grandeur and heartrending tenderness. Perhaps the saying is true: Fortune does indeed favor the brave.

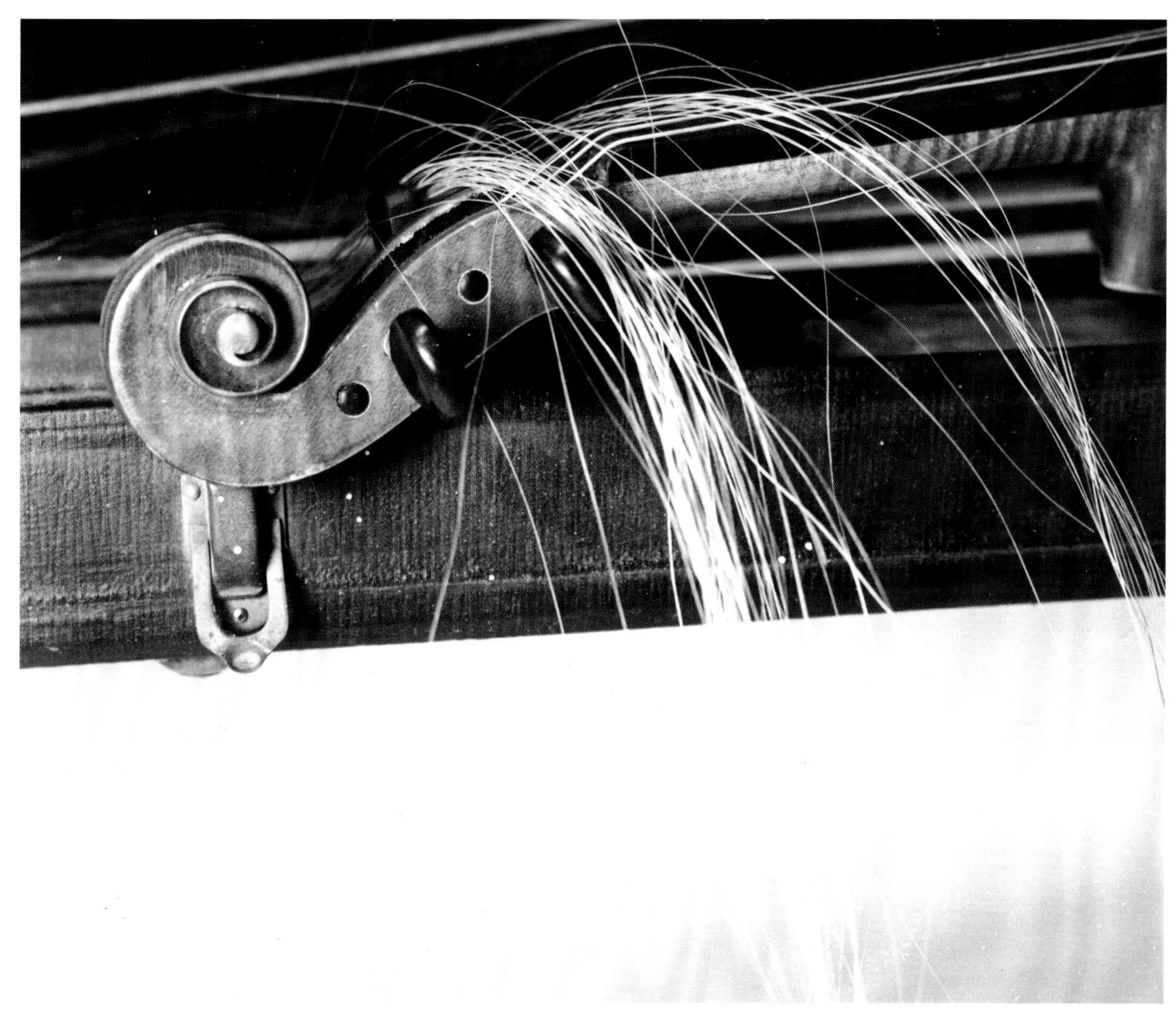

Untitled, 1971

Notes

1   Jay DeFeo, artist's statement in *Sixteen Americans,* exh. cat. (New York: The Museum of Modern Art, 1959), 8.

2   Bruce Conner, interview with Peter Boswell, June 15, 1983, cited in Boswell, "Theater of Light and Sound," *2000BC: The Bruce Conner Story Part II*, exh. cat. (Minneapolis: Walker Art Center, 1999), 41.

3   A rare exception is a group of painted portraits she made of Wallace Berman in 1974, which now reside in the collection of the Whitney Museum of American Art, New York.

4   Jay DeFeo, "Statement of Visual Concerns," unpublished notes, 1984; Doc0003, Archives of The Jay DeFeo Foundation, Berkeley.

5   "I don't think of myself as a 'representational artist' although occasionally recognizable representational forms occur. When they do they function more as 'symbol'—as in the eyes, or in the little vase of daisies (Fred's work) that I specifically call 'figure in landscape'" (Ibid.).

6   When asked about assemblage in her 1950s work, DeFeo said: "You know I always think of that as being such a strong part of my sensibility, and then when we get down to the bare facts, we don't really have much evidence of it." Jay DeFeo, interview with Sidra Stich, August 18, 1988; audio recording, Archives of The Jay DeFeo Foundation.

7   Ibid. The large-scale decorations she made for the 1964 San Francisco Art Institute's Artists' Ball were captured in a photograph that is now in the Nell Sinton papers in the Archives of American Art. Wall decorations created by Jay DeFeo for the San Francisco Art Institute's Artists' Ball, 1964 / unidentified photographer. Nell (Eleanor) and Stanley Sinton papers, [circa 1920]–1993. Archives of American Art, Smithsonian Institution, Washington, DC (Digital ID: 14000).

8   Jay DeFeo, lecture at Mills College, December 2, 1986; video recording, Archives of The Jay DeFeo Foundation.

9   To be, or not to be– that is the question:
    Whether 'tis nobler in the mind to suffer
    The slings and arrows of outrageous fortune
    Or to take arms against a sea of troubles,
    And by opposing end them. To die– to sleep–
    No more; and by a sleep to say we end

The heartache, and the thousand natural shocks
    That flesh is heir to. 'Tis a consummation
    Devoutly to be wish'd. To die– to sleep.
    To sleep– perchance to dream: ay, there's the rub!
    For in that sleep of death what dreams may come
    When we have shuffled off this mortal coil,
    Must give us pause.

10 Jay DeFeo, lecture at University of California, Santa Cruz, May 10, 1989; video recording, Archives of The Jay DeFeo Foundation.

11 Ibid.

12 Jay DeFeo, letter to Astrea Mateos, 1961; Corr0583, Archives of The Jay DeFeo Foundation.

13 Jay DeFeo, interview with Paul Karlstrom, June 3, 1975 (Session 1). Archives of American Art, Smithsonian Institution, Washington, DC (recorded at the artist's home in Larkspur, California).

14 Jay DeFeo, interview with Sidra Stich, September 16, 1988; audio recording, Archives of The Jay DeFeo Foundation.

15 Jay DeFeo, journal entry, October 15, 1975; Doc0007, Archives of The Jay DeFeo Foundation.

16 Jay DeFeo, interview with Sidra Stich, October 9, 1988; audio recording, Archives of The Jay DeFeo Foundation.

17 My hunch that the work was initially intended as a portrait is based on the title *Traveling Portrait (Chance Landscape)*. But I would argue that this was intended as a symbolic portrait, using her teeth to form one or more floral shapes. This would be supported by a journal entry from about this same time: "more cutting – perhaps a landscape of teeth – or explosion of roses." Jay DeFeo, journal entry, May 10, 1973; Doc0005, Archives of The Jay DeFeo Foundation.

18 DeFeo described these circumstances as a moth deciding to "commit suicide." Jay DeFeo, lecture at San Francisco Art Institute, February 11, 1978; audio recording, Archives of The Jay DeFeo Foundation.

19 Jay DeFeo, letter to Ed Kienholz, September 9, 1979; Corr1146, Archives of The Jay DeFeo Foundation.

20   Corey Keller mentions Breton and the magical circumstantial in "My Favorite Things: The Photographs of Jay DeFeo," *Jay DeFeo: A Retrospective*, exh. cat. (New York: Whitney Museum of American Art, 2012), 75. If one considers the moth a found object (although in this case it would be a reverse-engineered found object), one could argue that the work demonstrates elements of the magical circumstantial as well.

21   Jay DeFeo, interview with Paul Karlstrom, July 18, 1975 (Session 2); transcript of audiotaped interview, Archives of American Art, Smithsonian Institution, Washington, DC, 2, 9.

22   It is interesting to note that a decade later DeFeo referenced another fairy tale, *Snow White and the Seven Dwarfs*, in seven drawings she made of her rubber galoshes, each named for a dwarf.

23   Bruce Conner, interview with the author and Leah Levy, February 20, 2007, San Francisco; transcript in the archives of the Whitney Museum of American Art, New York.

24   Comte de Lautréamont (pseudonym for Isidore Ducasse), *Les Chants de Maldoror* (Paris: Gustave Balitout, Questroy et Cie, 1868–69).

25   Jay DeFeo, journal entry, December 3, 1973; Doc0004, Archives of The Jay DeFeo Foundation.

26   When asked in 1986 by a researcher if the "Free Association of Surrealism" was an influence, DeFeo responded simply "yes." Jay DeFeo, letter to Janet L. Zapata, March 23, 1986; Corr1178, Archives of The Jay DeFeo Foundation.

27   Jay DeFeo, letter to Robert Emory Johnson, September 25, 1974; Corr0679, original in private collection.

28   Jay DeFeo, statement prepared for Dorothy Miller, 1977; Doc00023, Archives of The Jay DeFeo Foundation.

29   Jay DeFeo, journal entry, May 24, 1975; Doc0007, Archives of The Jay DeFeo Foundation.

30   Nathan Cabot Hale, *Abstraction in Art and Nature: A Program of Study for Artists, Teachers, and Students* (New York: Watson-Guptil, 1972), 243.

31   "saw [William] Wiley show I understand the levels of his work – but still doesn't move me all that much. (The "Beauty must be convulsive" standard that Breton suggests to me.) – Bruce on the other hand provides convulsiveness for me! His angels are lovely. Am making some vacation collages & Xeroxing his angels." Jay DeFeo, journal entry, October 19, 1975; Doc0007, Archives of The Jay DeFeo Foundation.

32   Jay DeFeo, journal entry, January 25, 1976; Doc0008, Archives of The Jay DeFeo Foundation.

33   "Have done some small – not too good studies of the lamb bone – that changes every time R. Mutt finds it in an accessible place (Merz getting first one) associate this with Bruce's Angel collages." Jay DeFeo, journal entry, December 23, 1975; Doc0007, Archives of The Jay DeFeo Foundation.

34   Jay DeFeo, journal entry, November 7, 1975; Doc0007, Archives of The Jay DeFeo Foundation.

35   Jay DeFeo, lecture at Mills College, December 2 and 4, 1986; video recording, Archives of The Jay DeFeo Foundation.

36   Ibid.

37   See entry for Maenad of Skopas in the database of Museum of Classical Archaeology, University of Cambridge; http://museum.classics.cam.ac.uk/collections/casts/maenad-skopas, accessed October 15, 2017.

38   Al Morch, "The Prize Rebirth of an Abstractionist," *San Francisco Examiner*, April 23, 1984, B16. It seems unlikely that viewers would guess one of the sources for her imagery was the hats worn by the band Devo, which Conner had apparently mentioned to her.

39   Jay DeFeo, journal entry, August 1984; Doc0016, Archives of The Jay DeFeo Foundation.

40   Jay DeFeo in conversation with Leah Levy, 1988, as recounted to the author, October 2017.

41   Jay DeFeo, letter to Henry Hopkins, June 21, 1978; Corr0564, Archives of The Jay DeFeo Foundation.

Plates

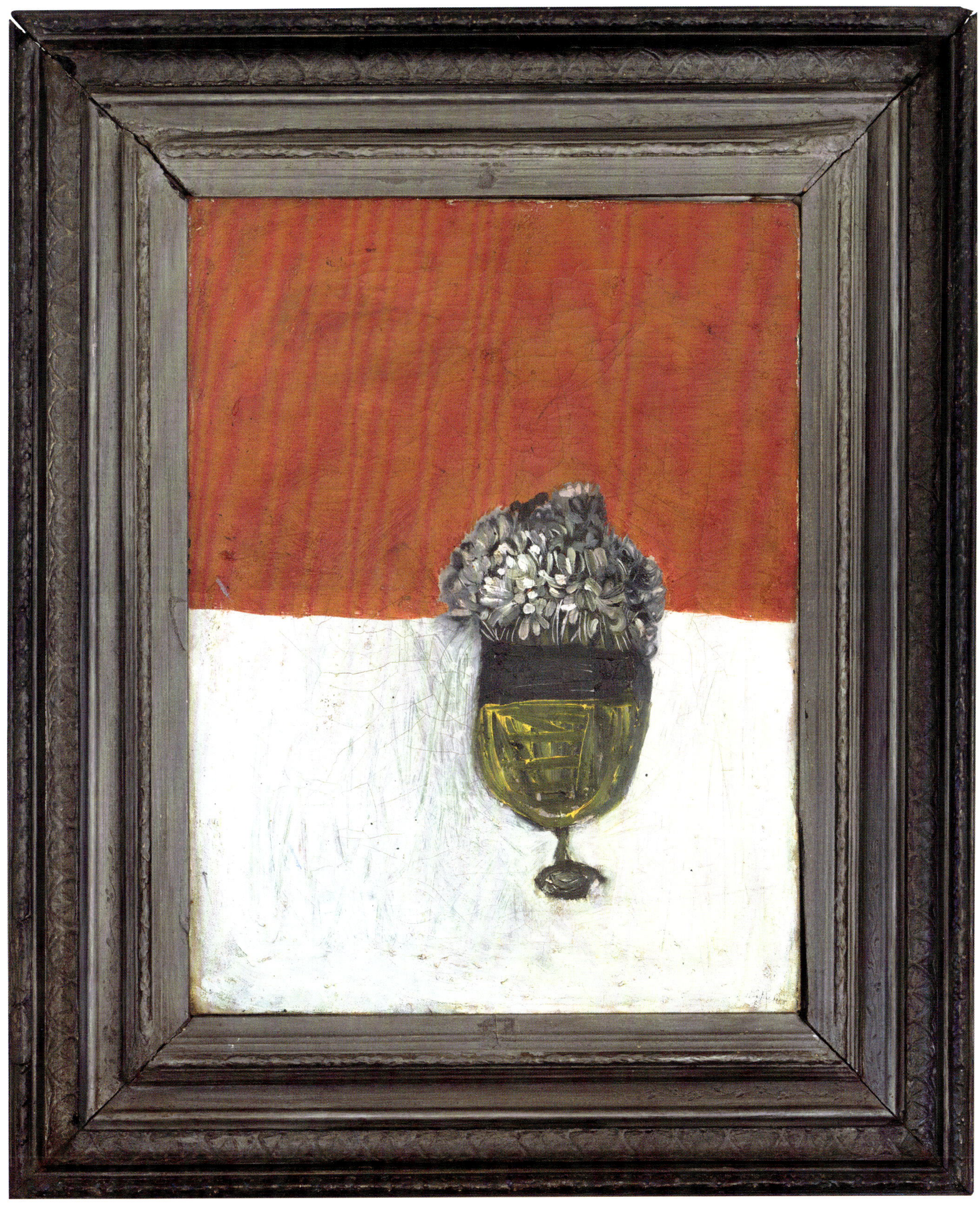

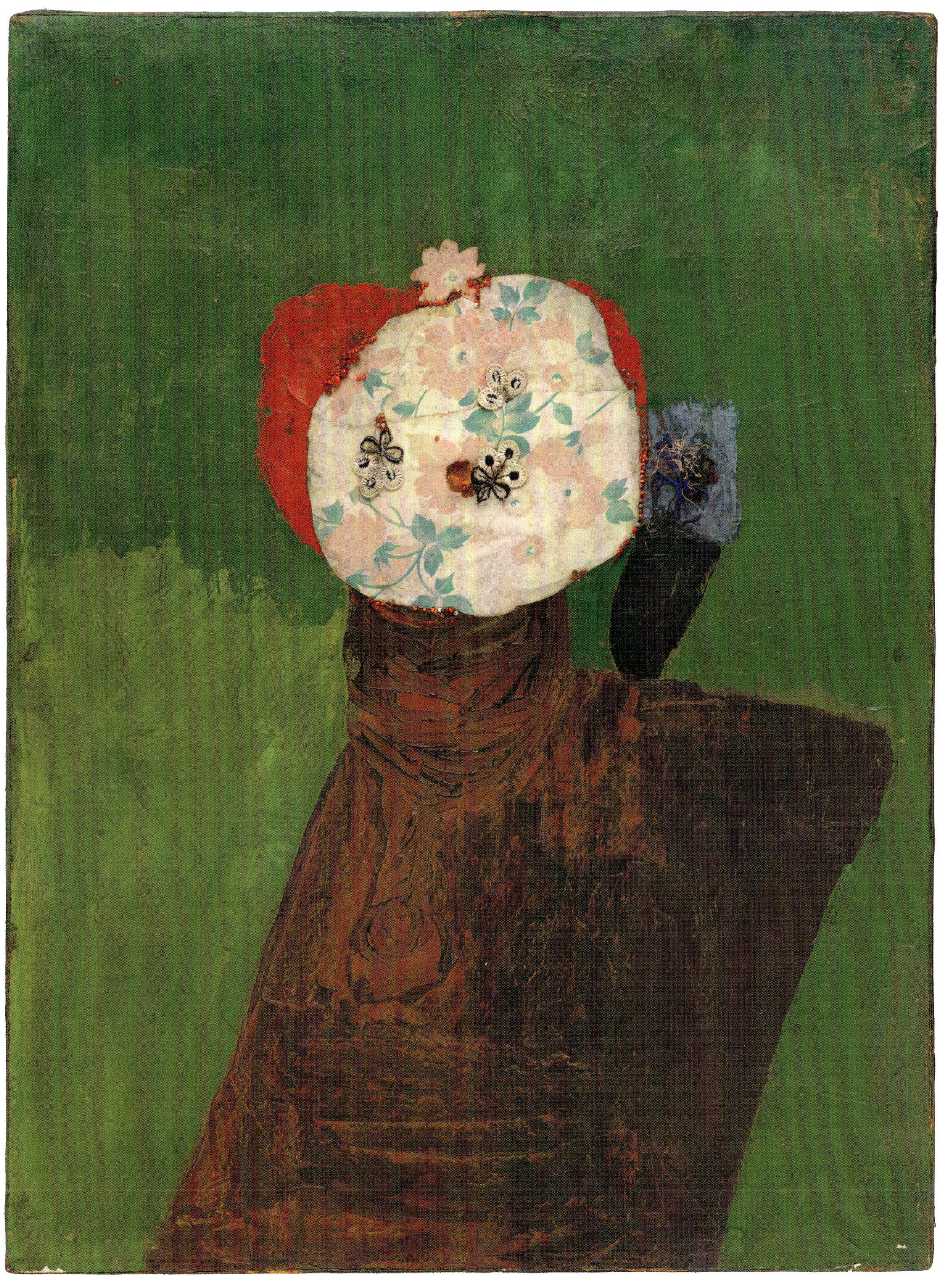

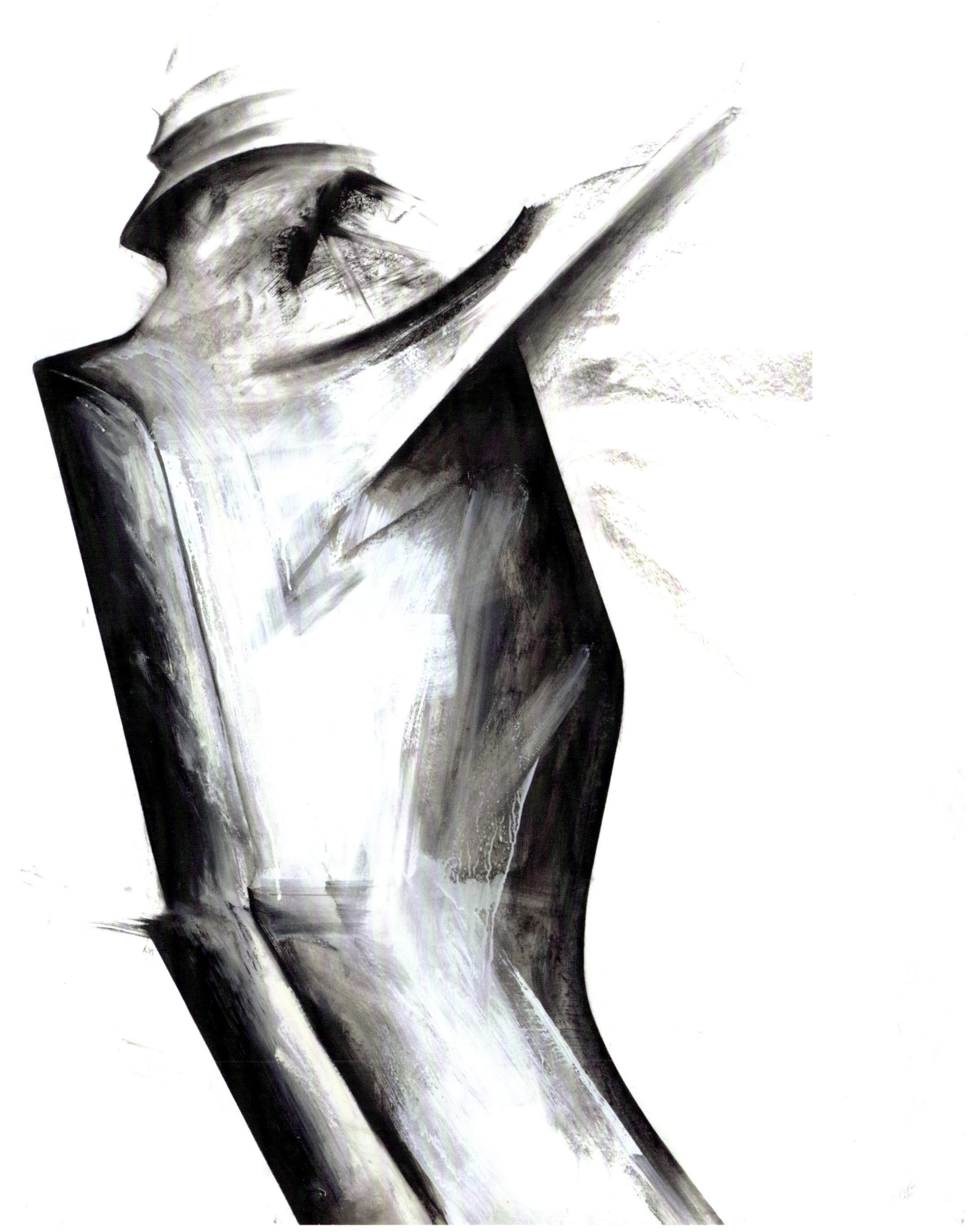

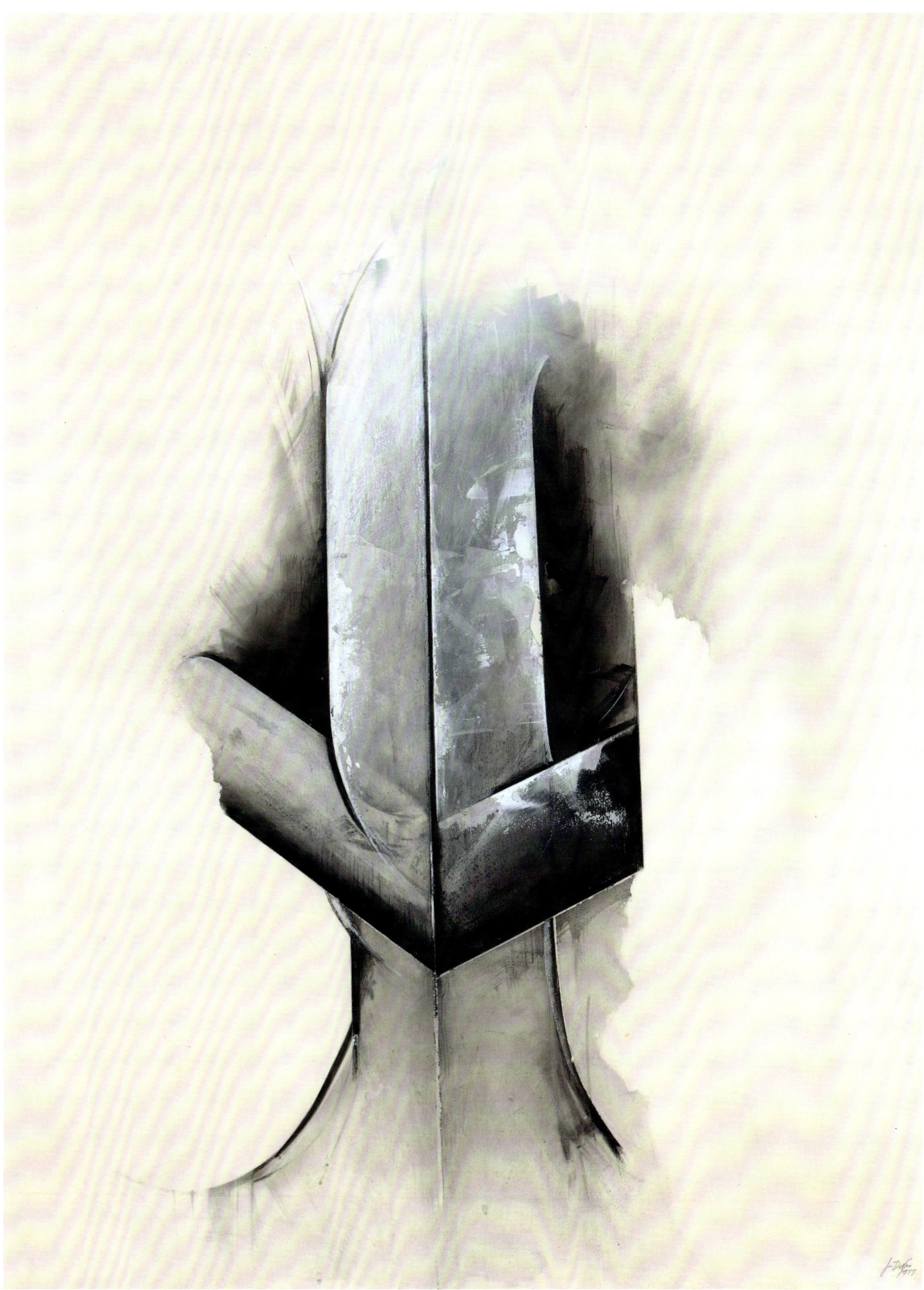

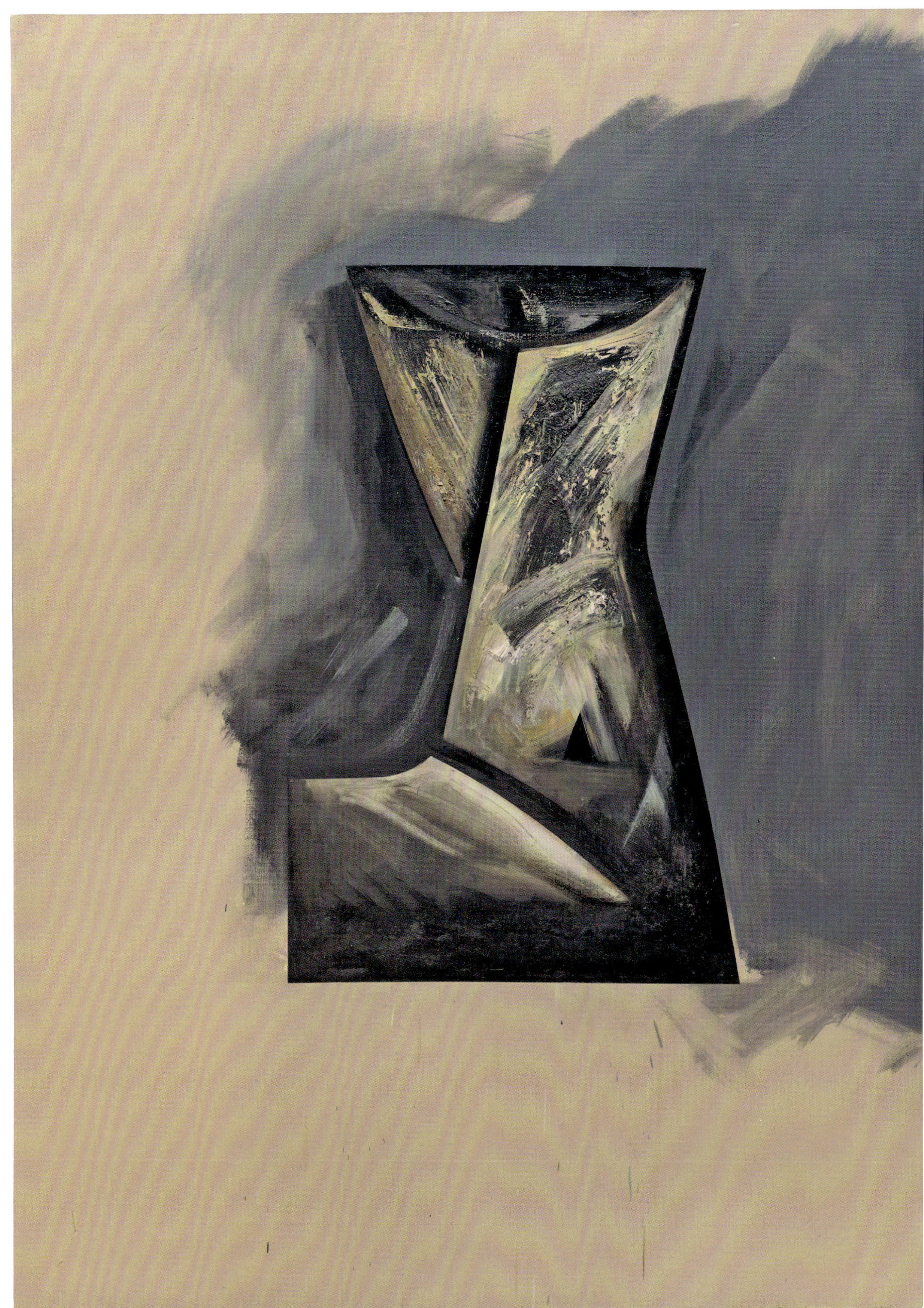

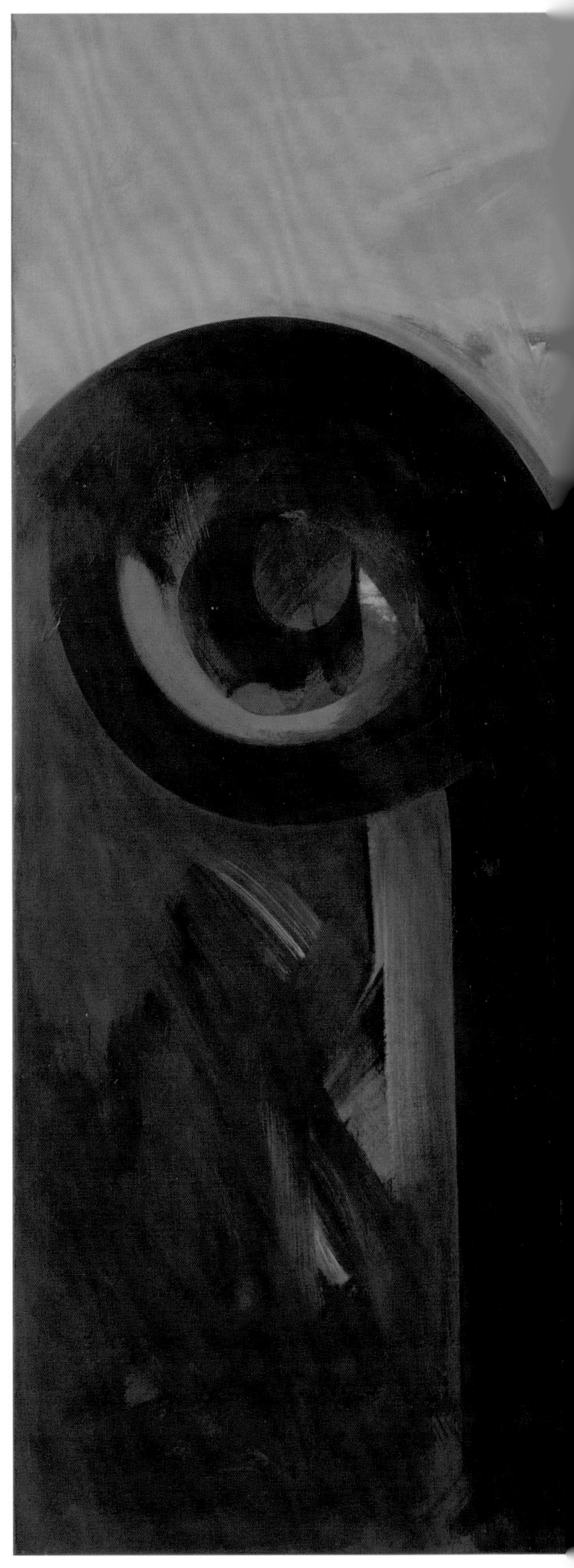

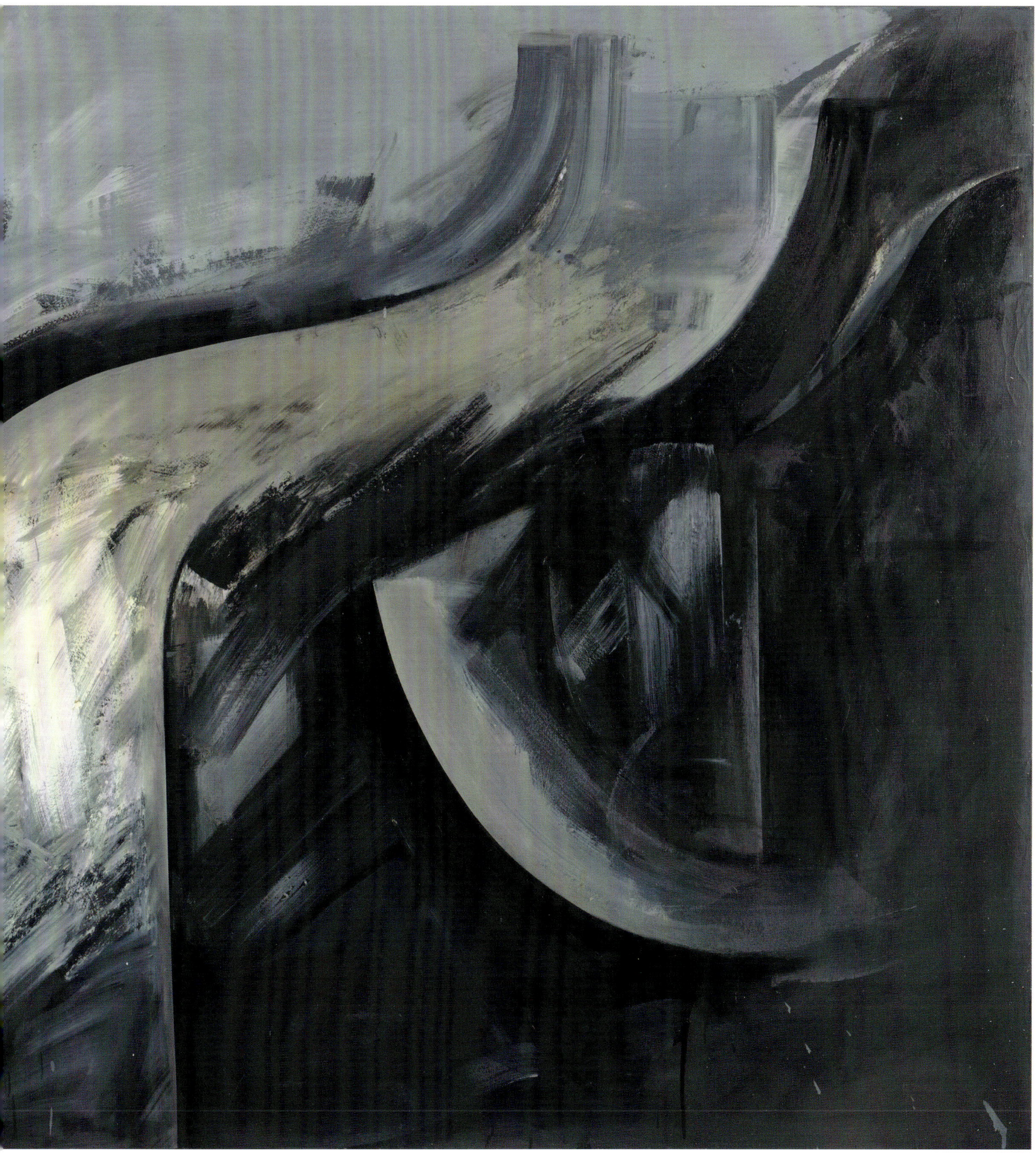

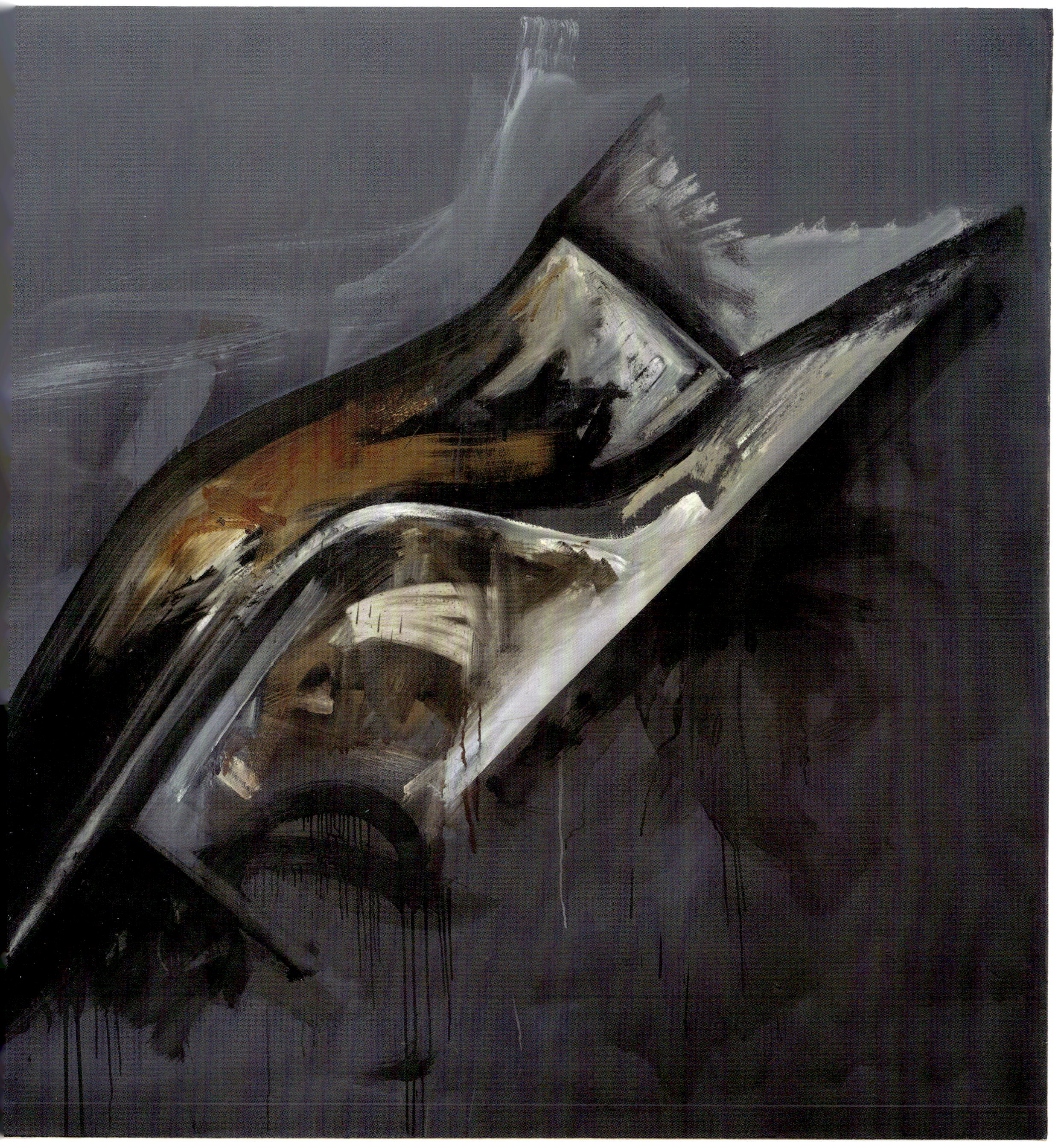

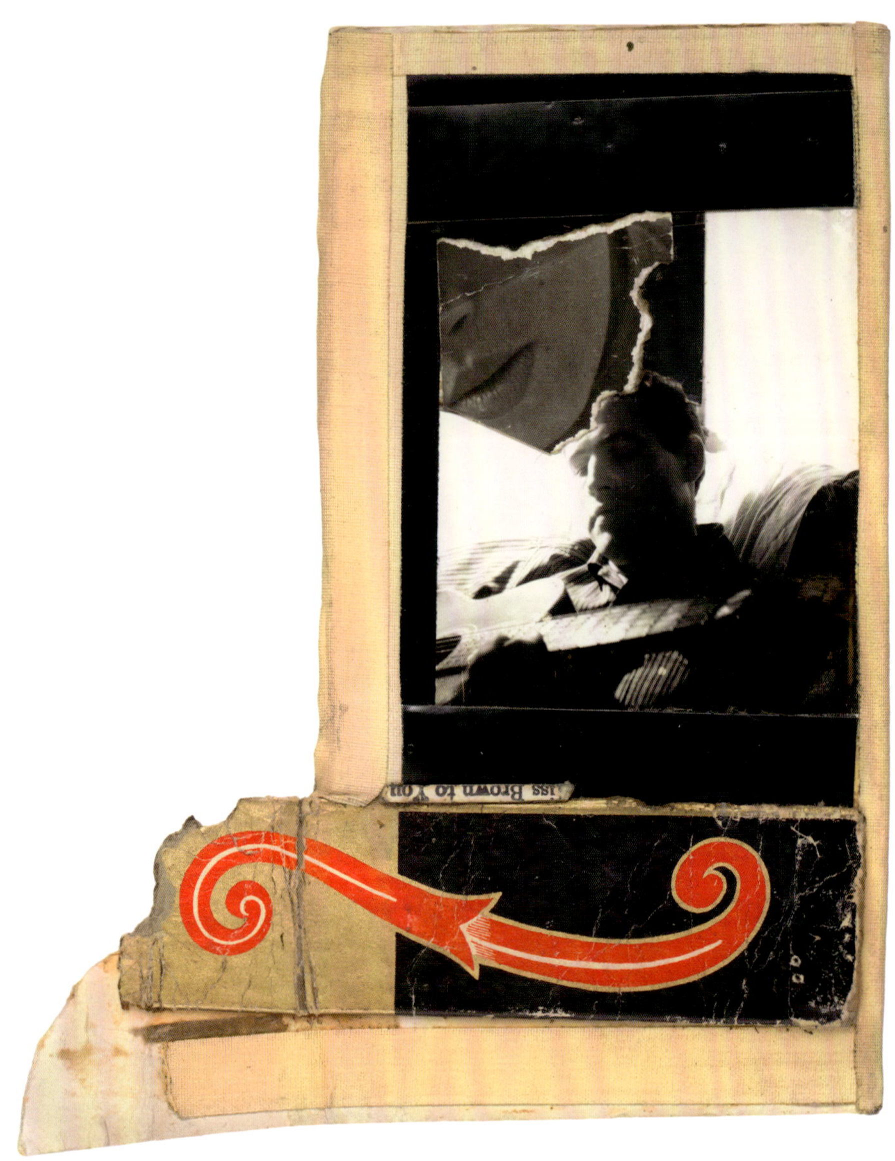
iss Brown to You

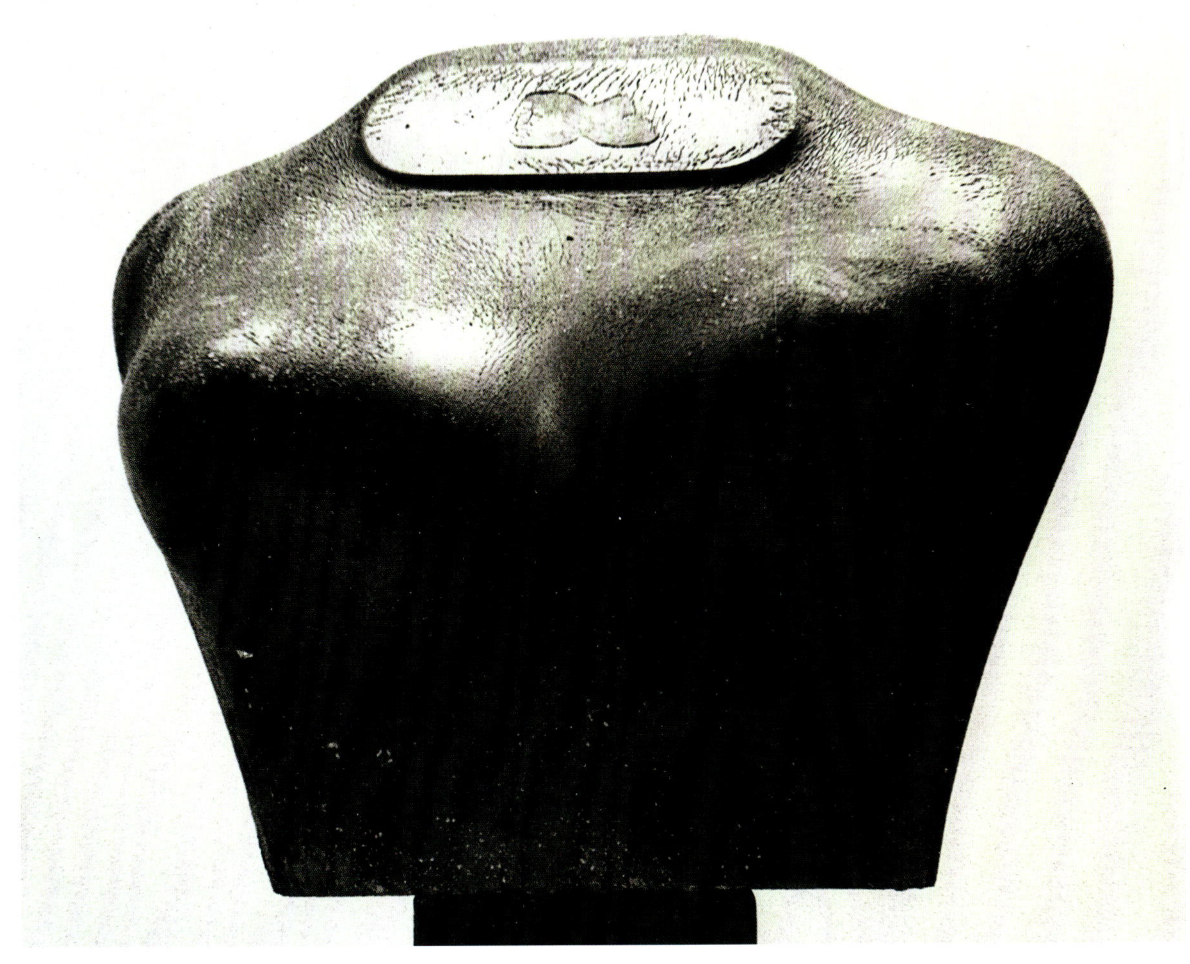

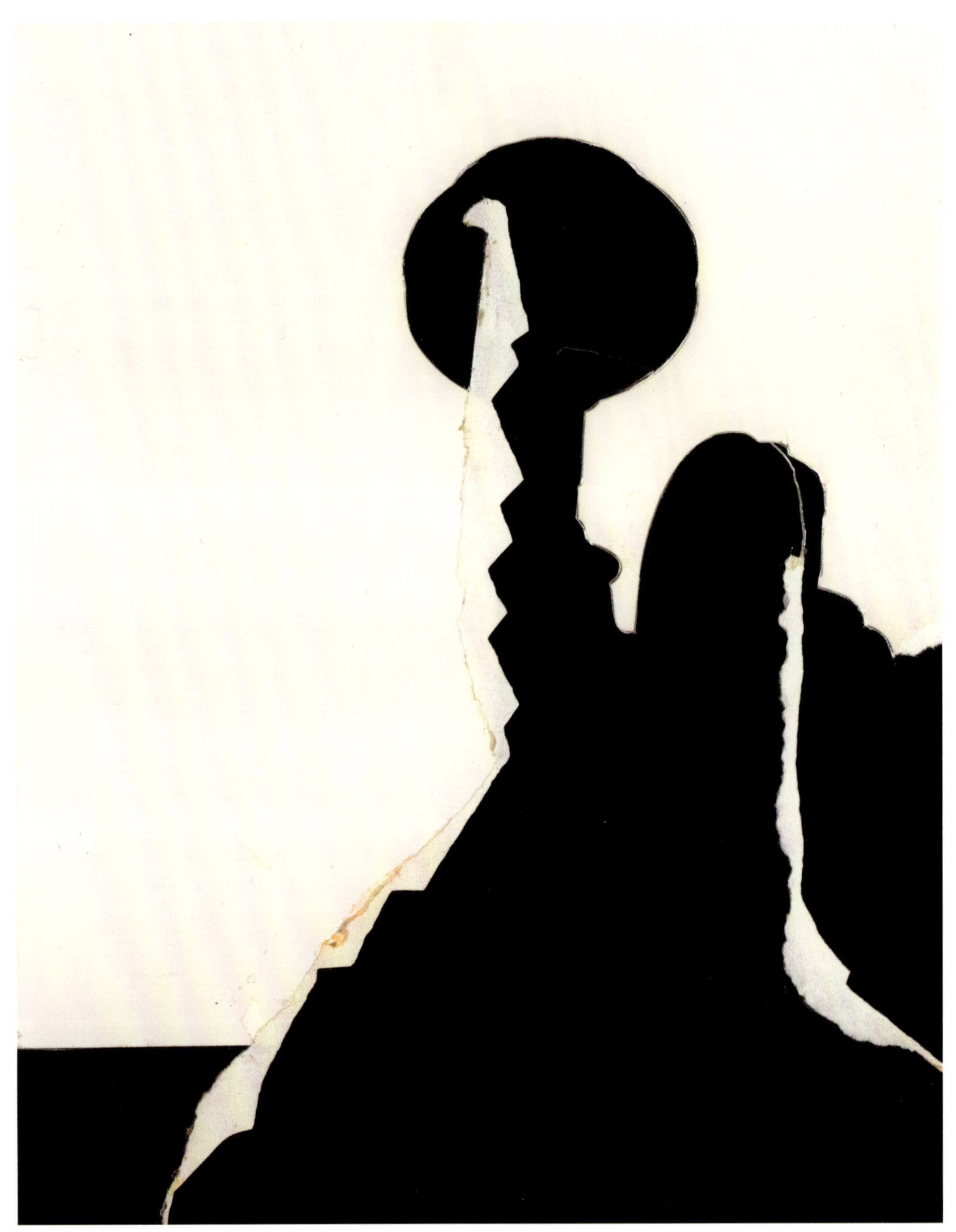

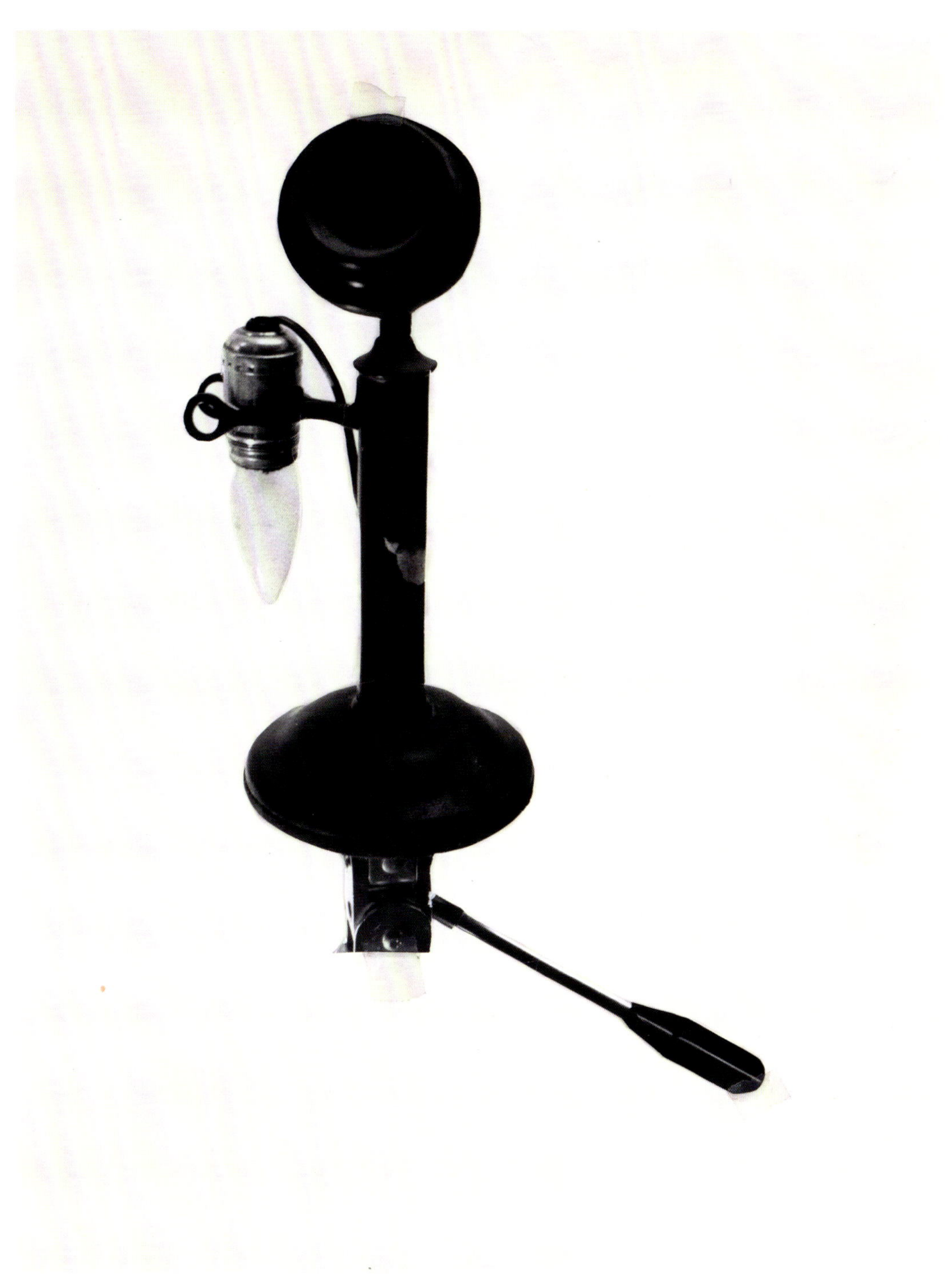

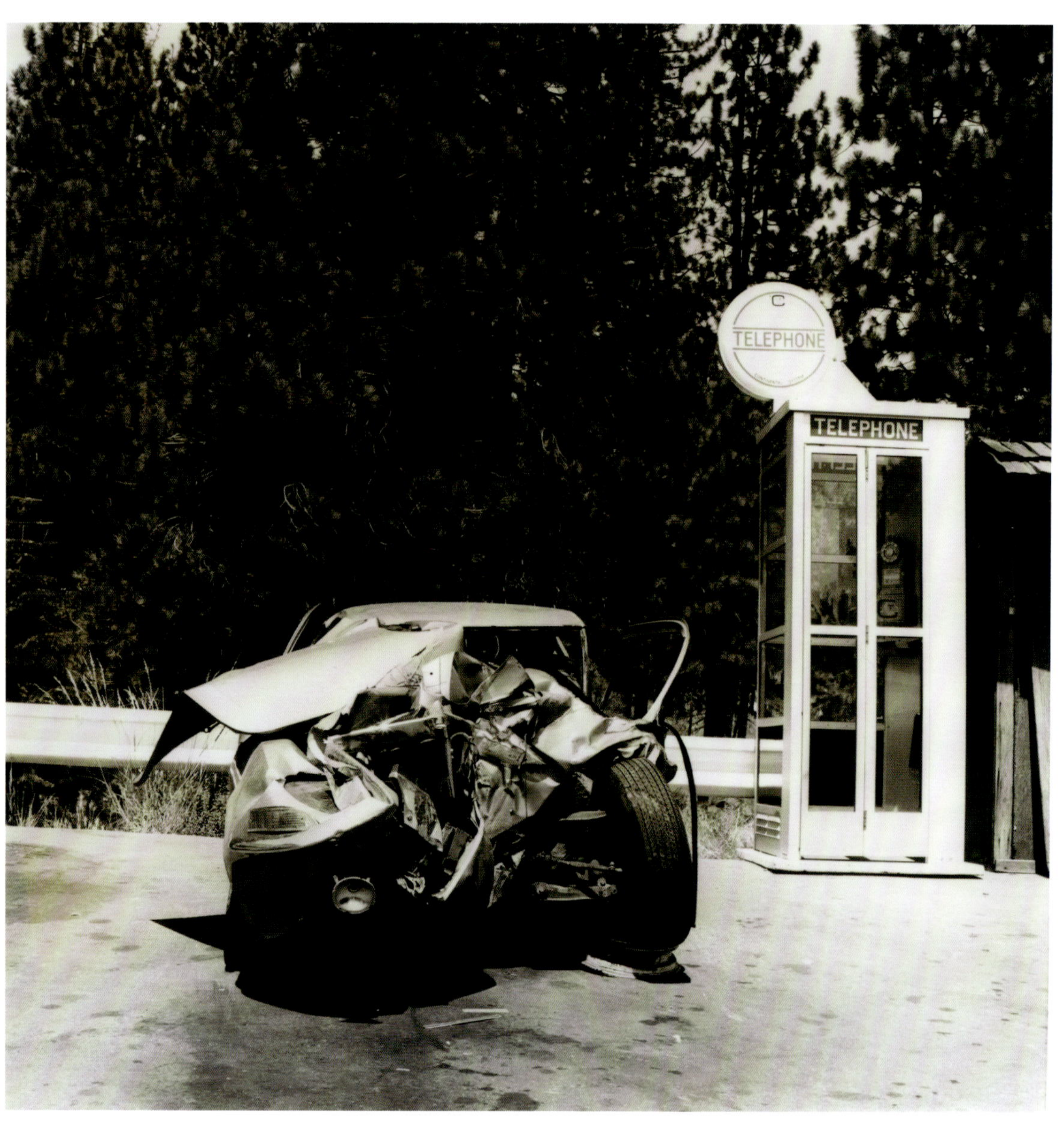

TELEPHONE
TELEPHONE

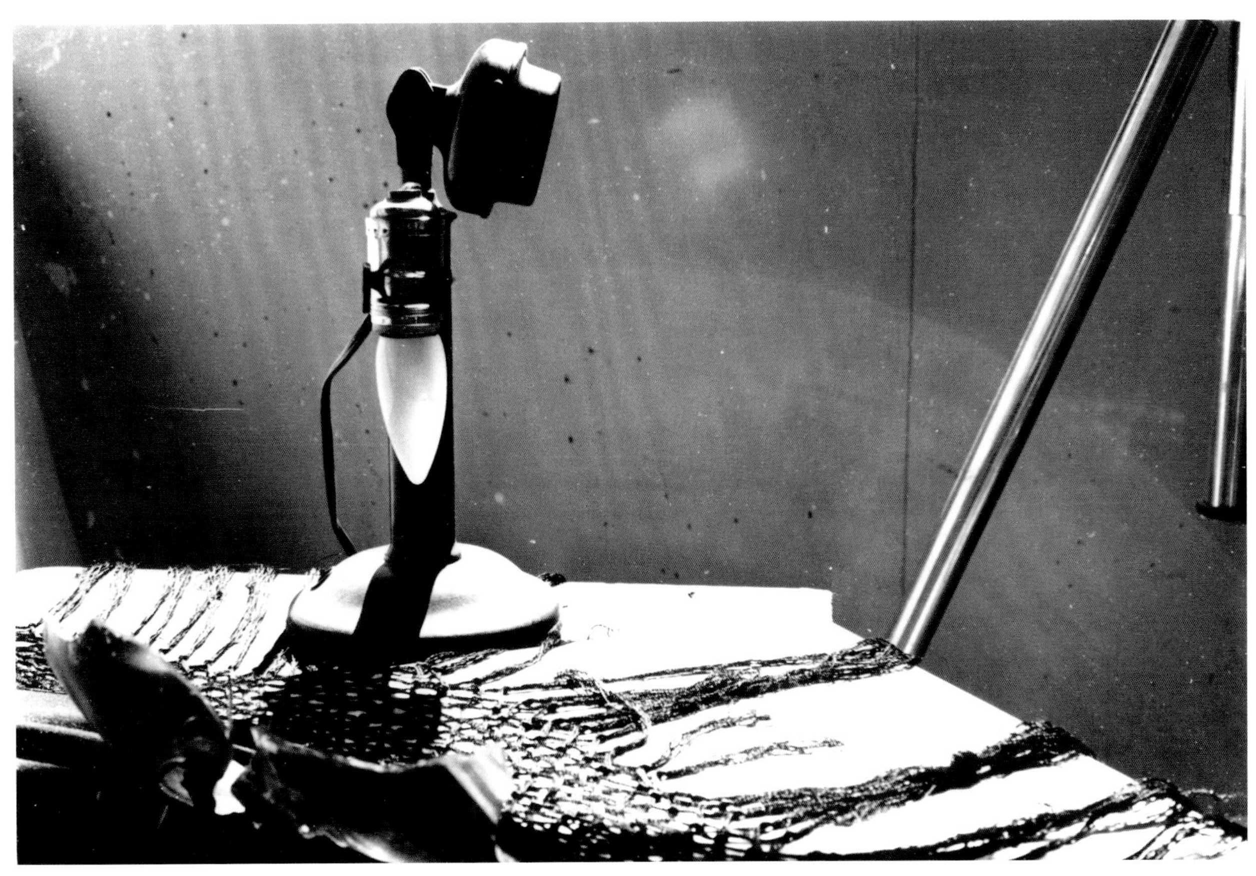

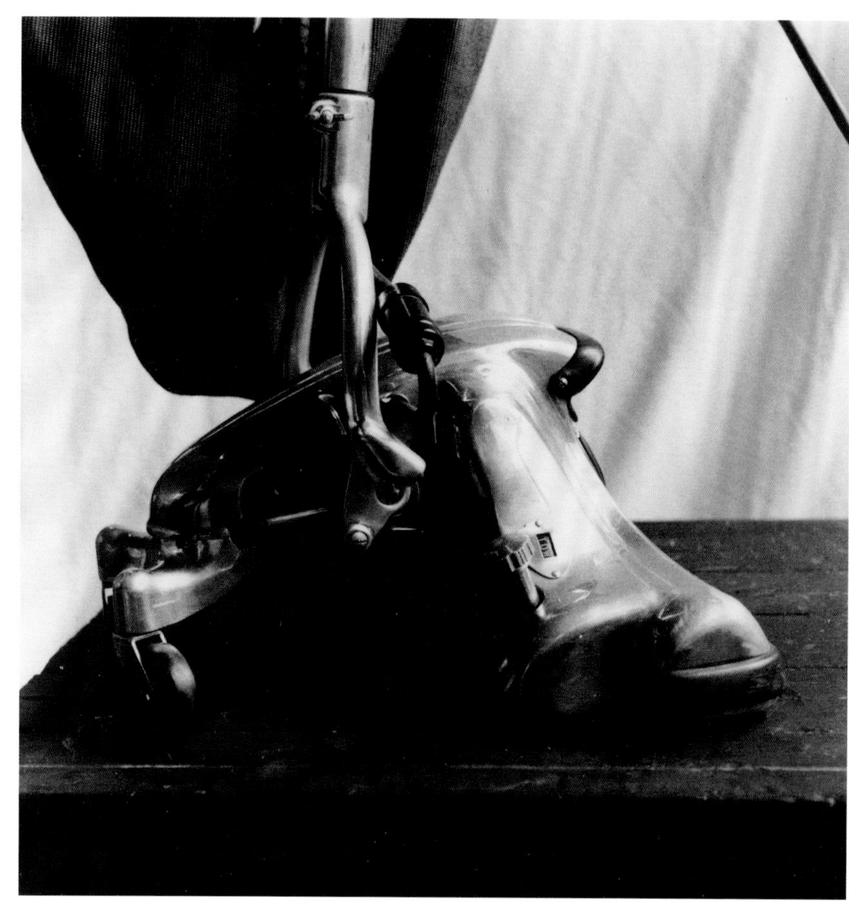

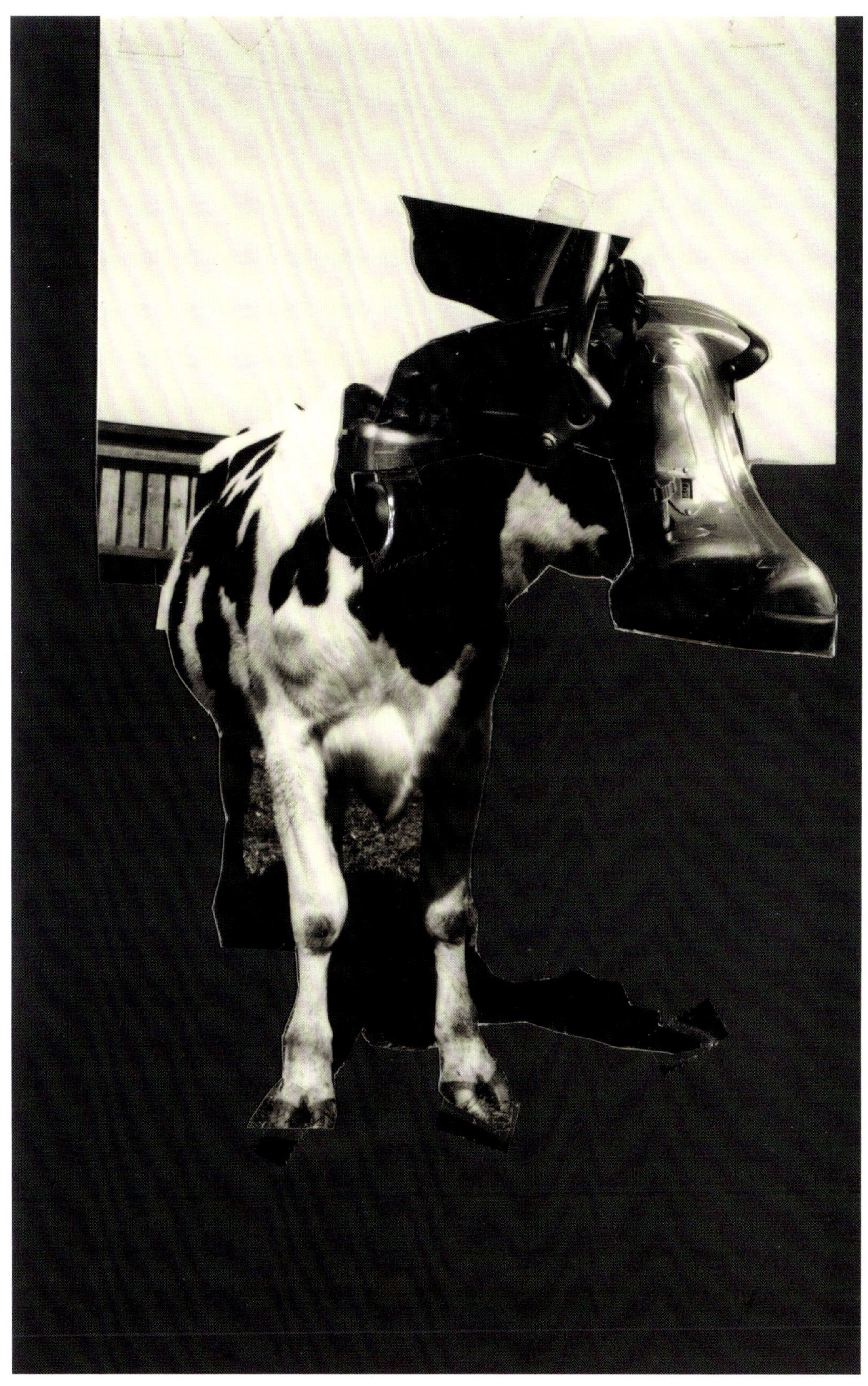

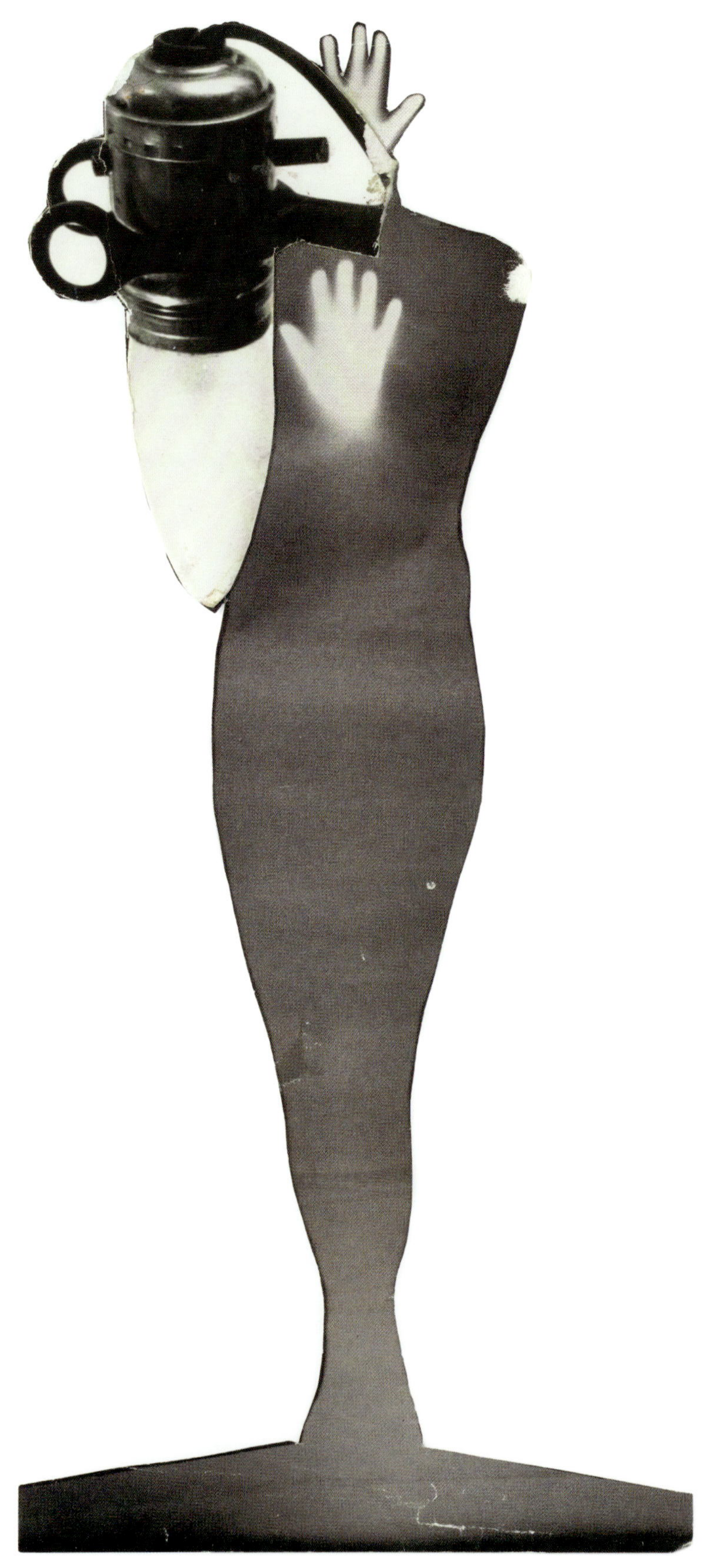

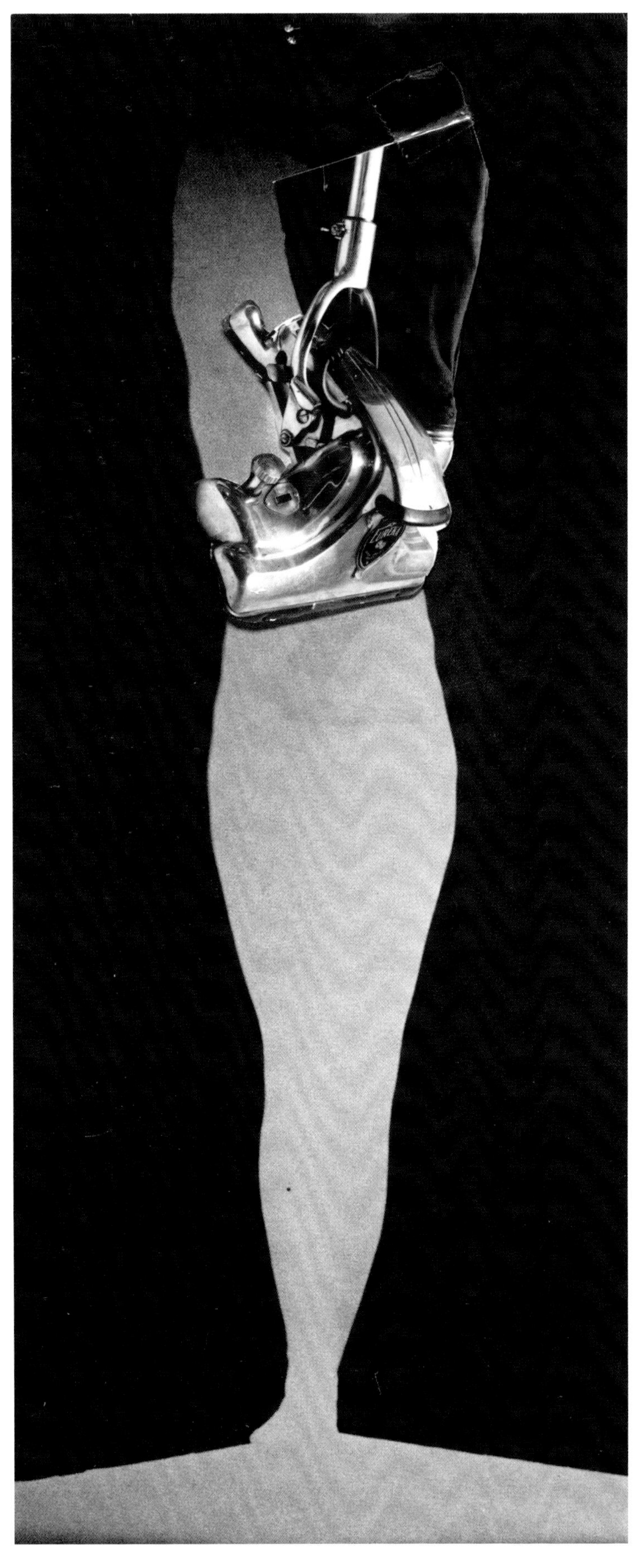

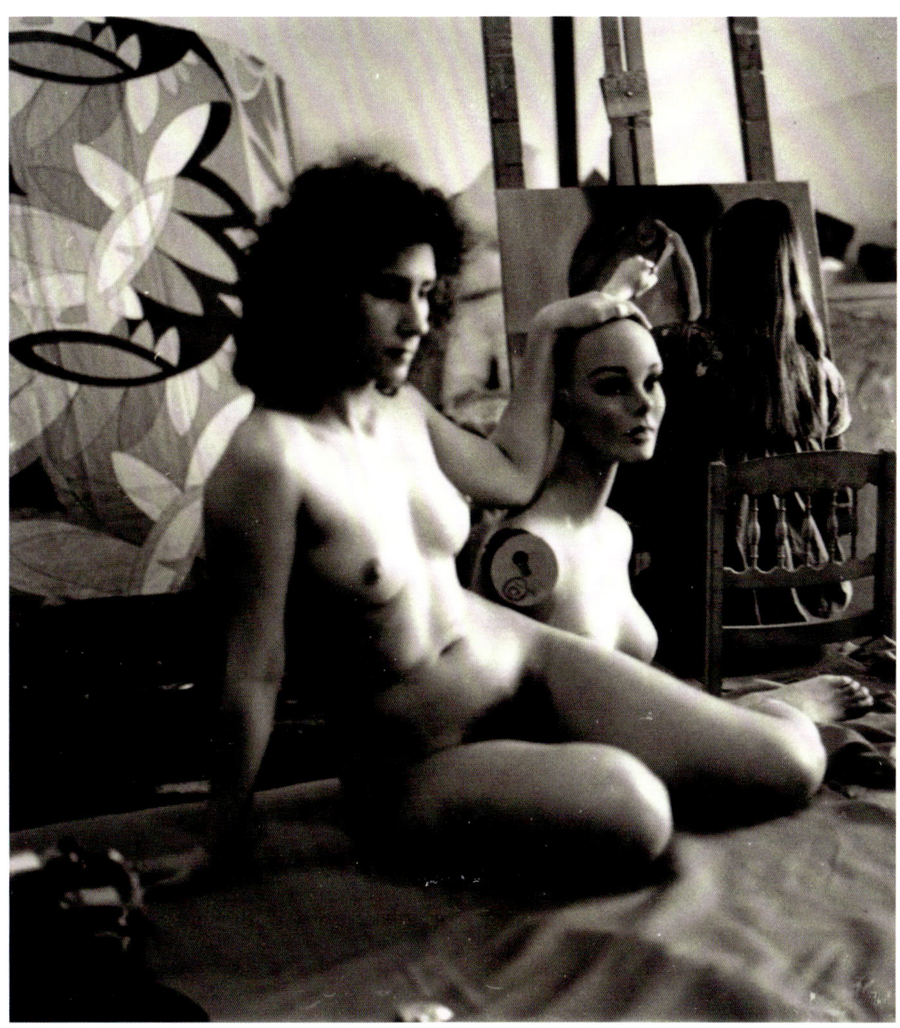

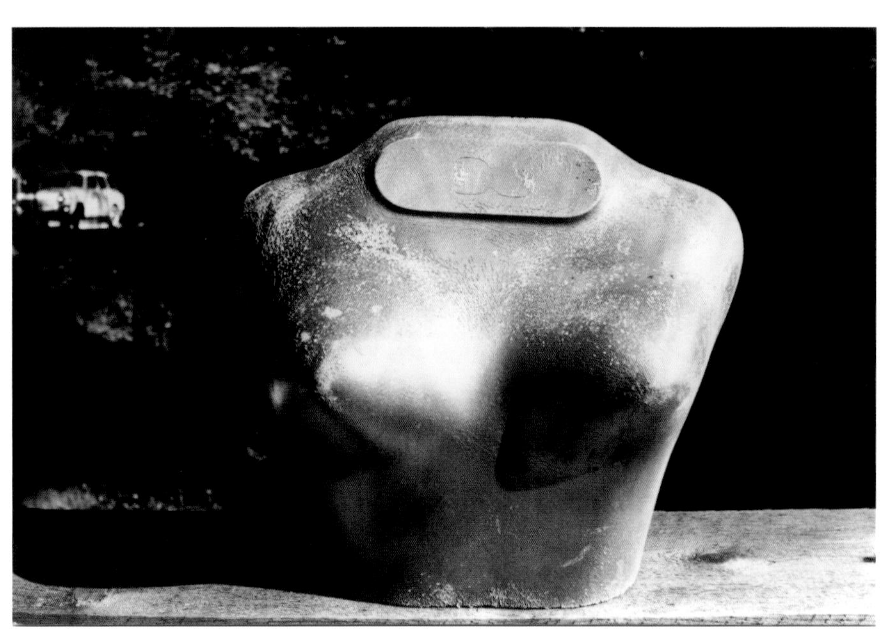

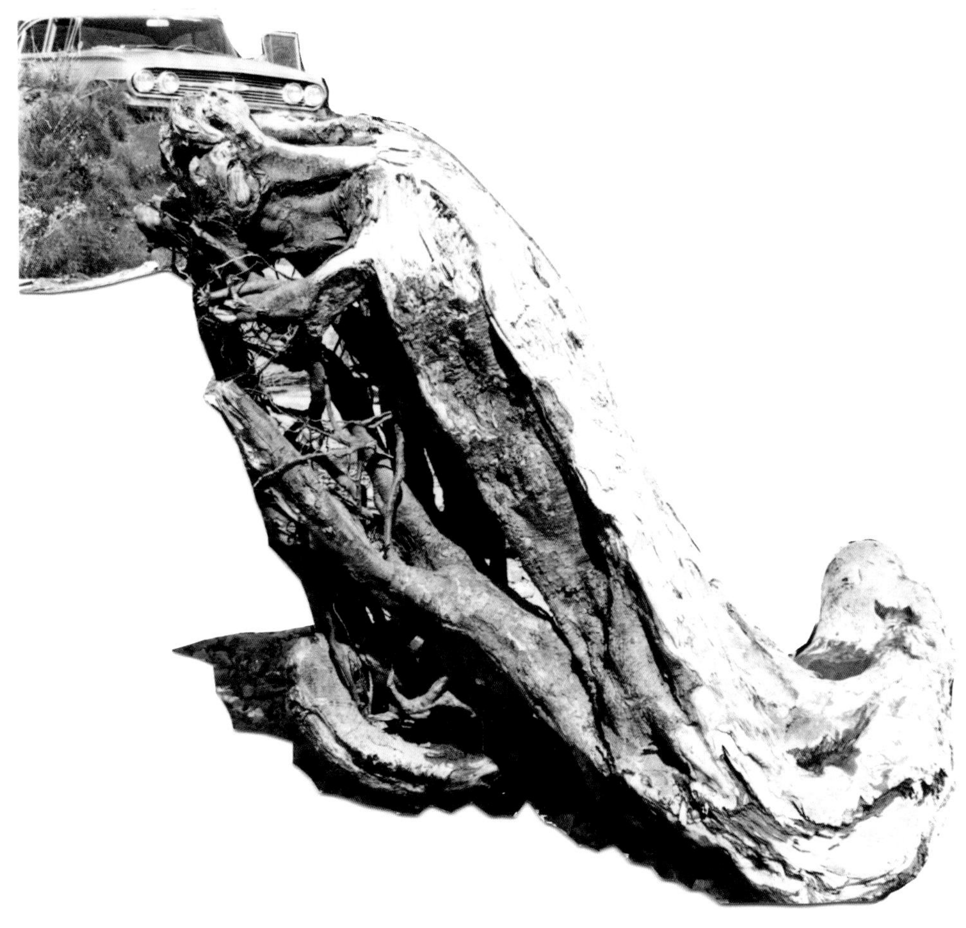

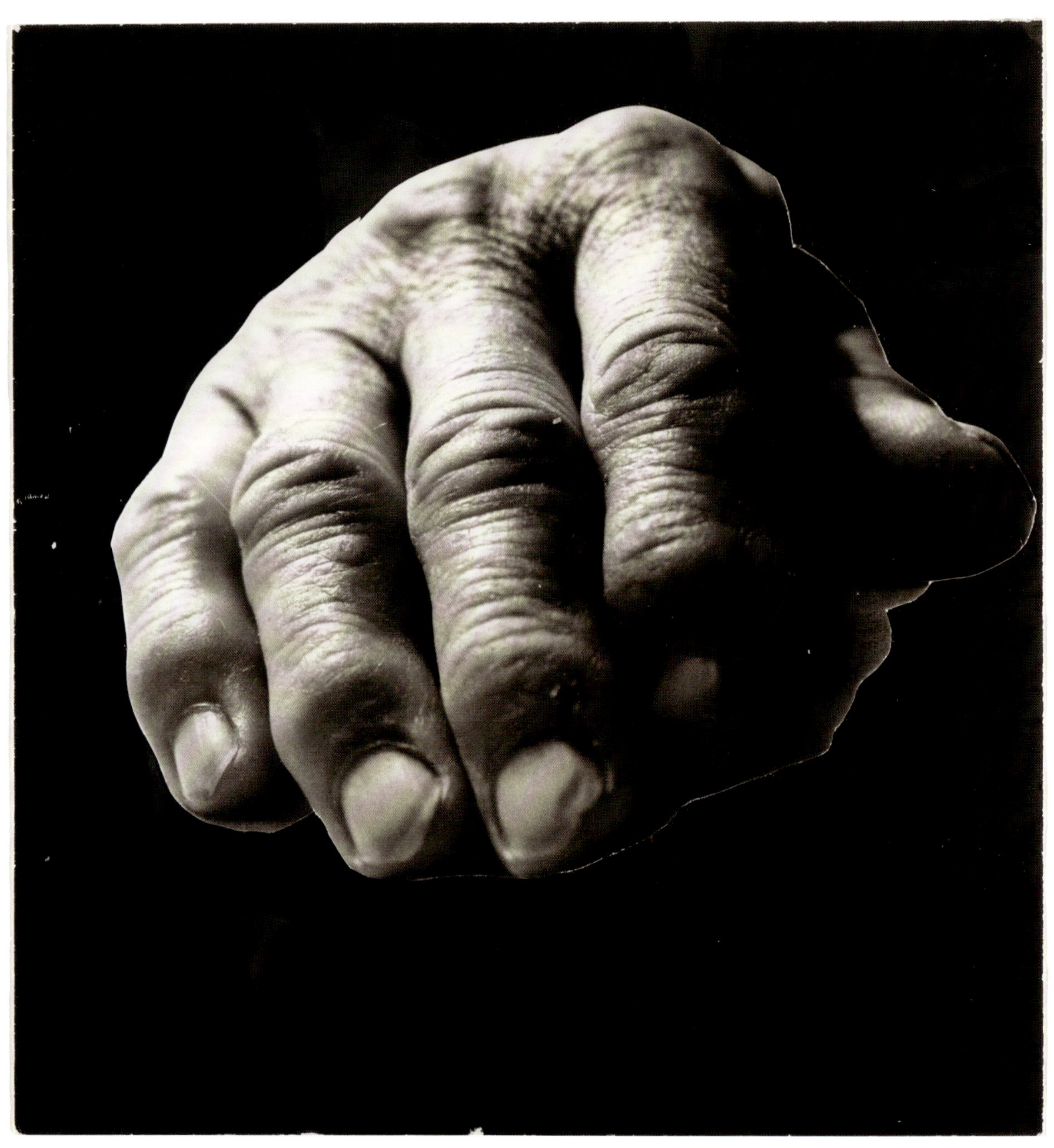

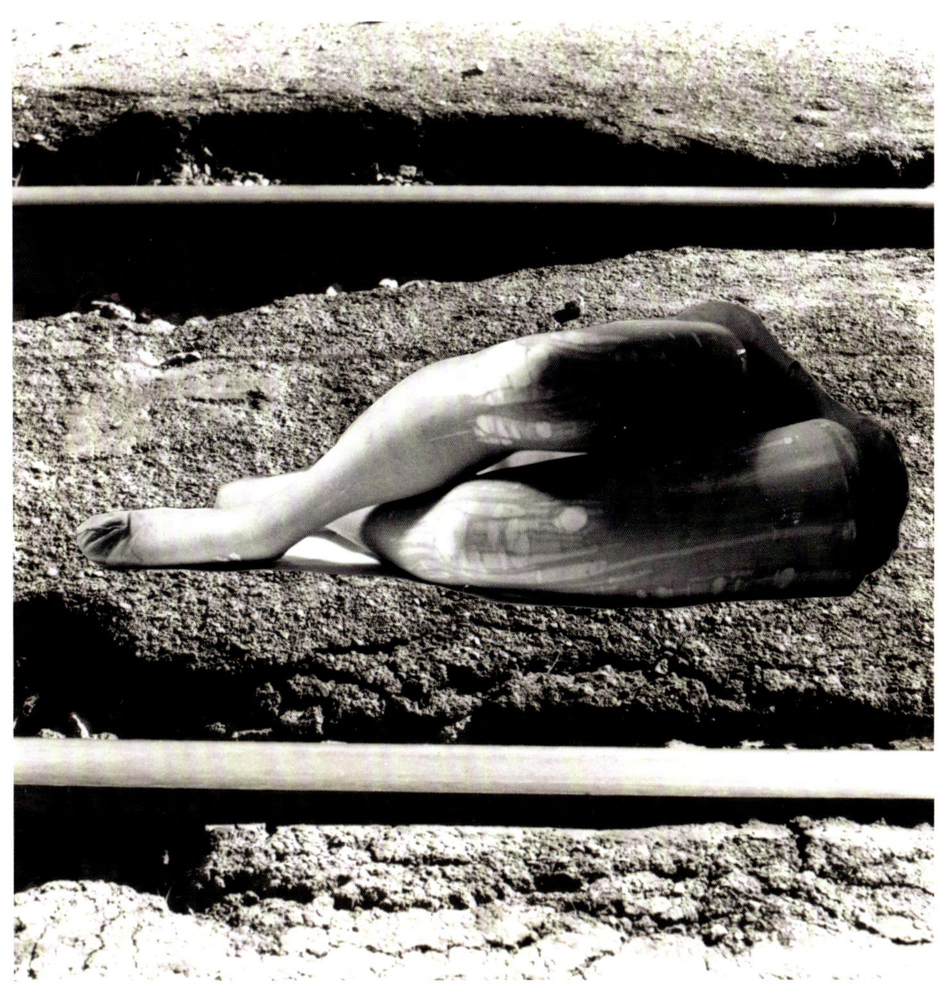

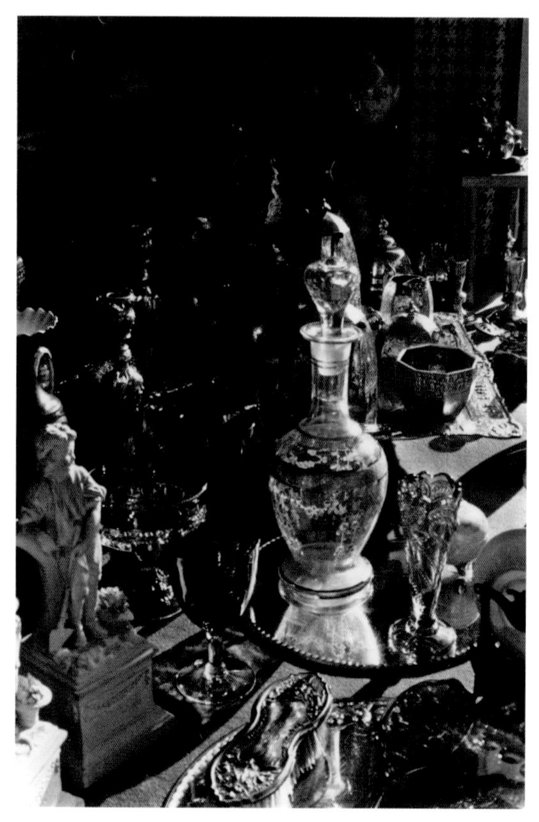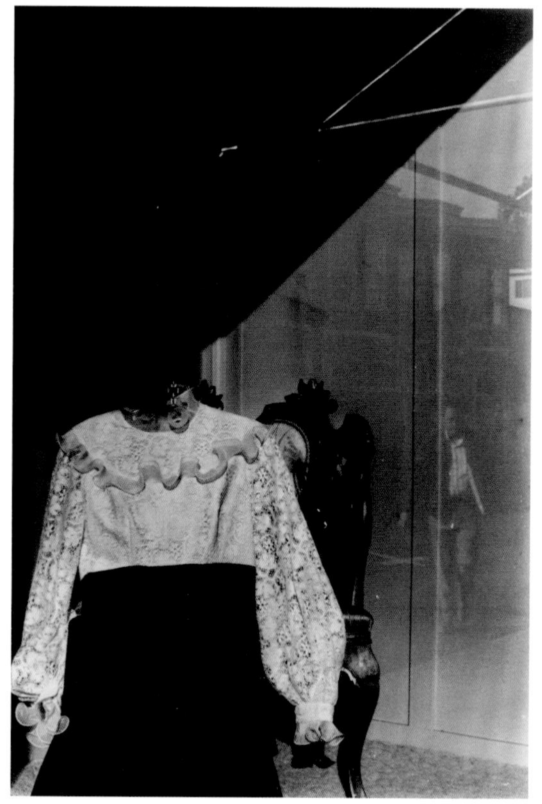

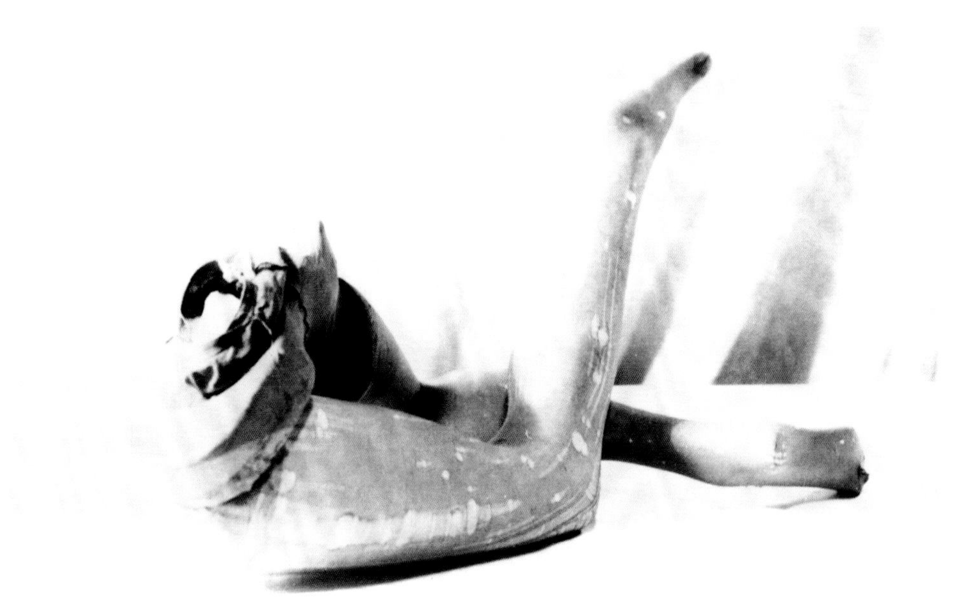

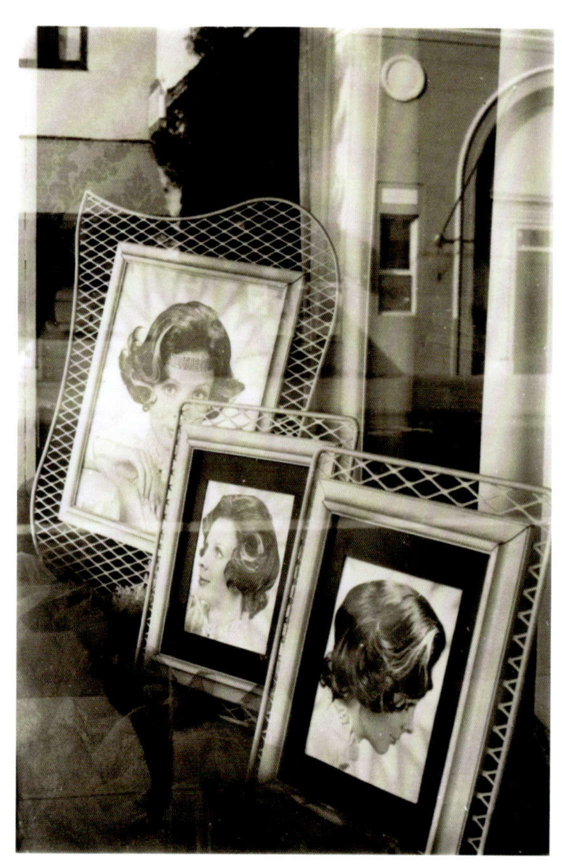

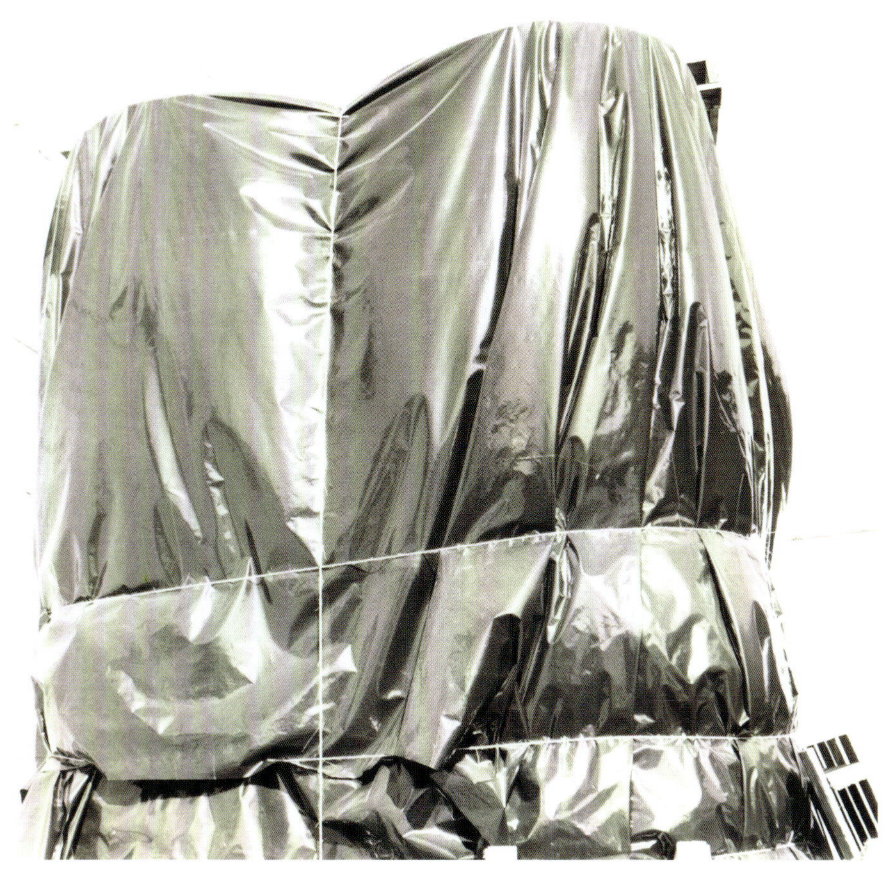

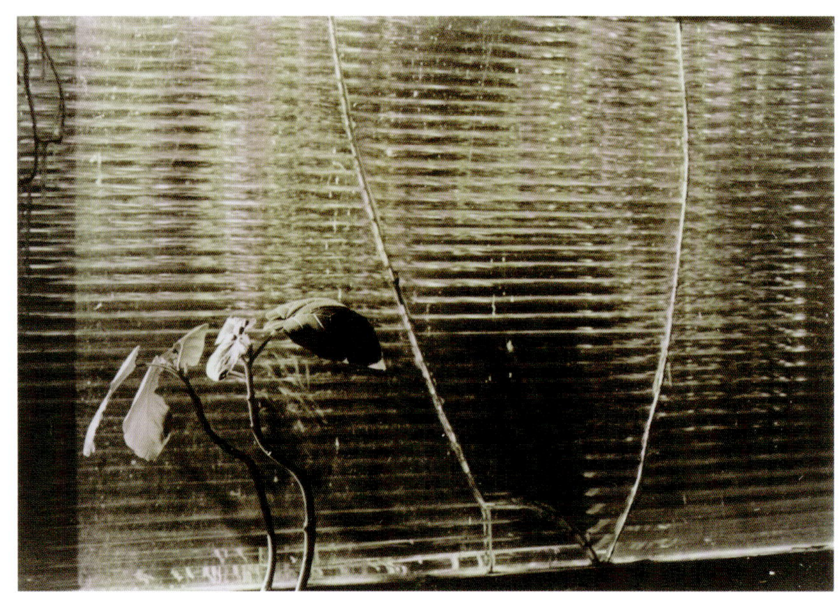

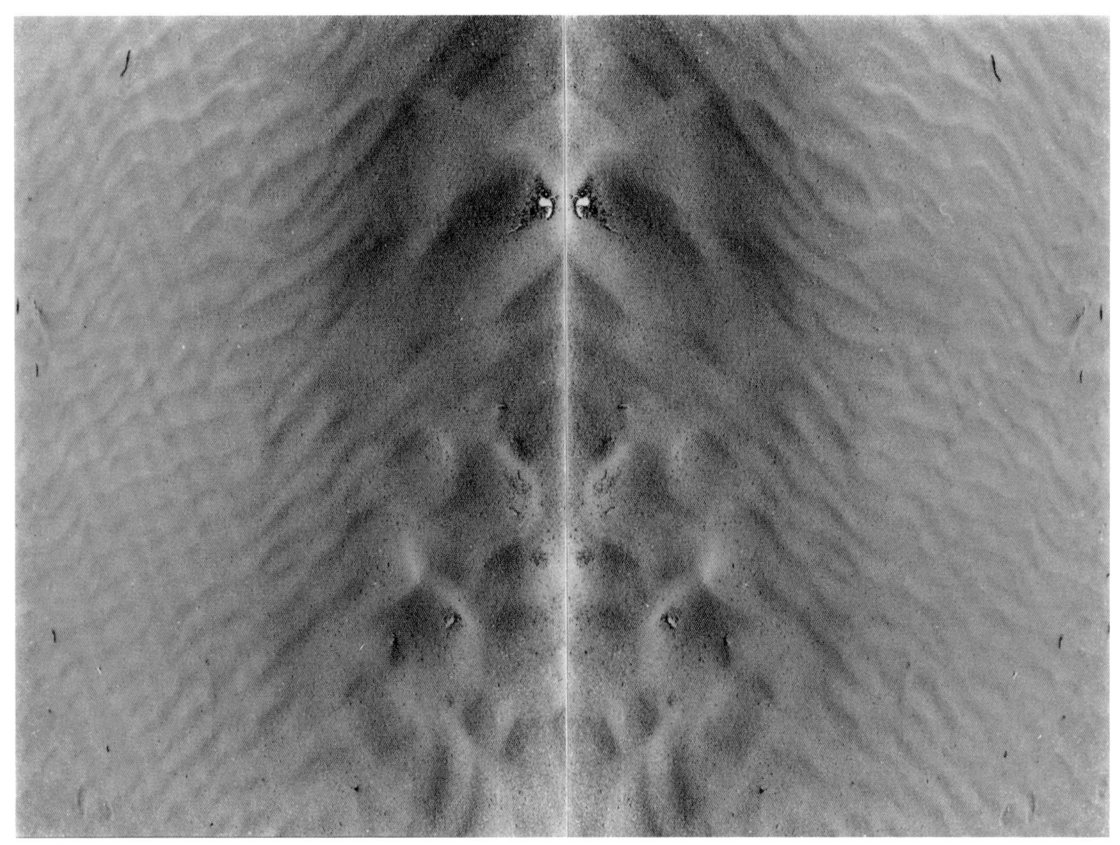

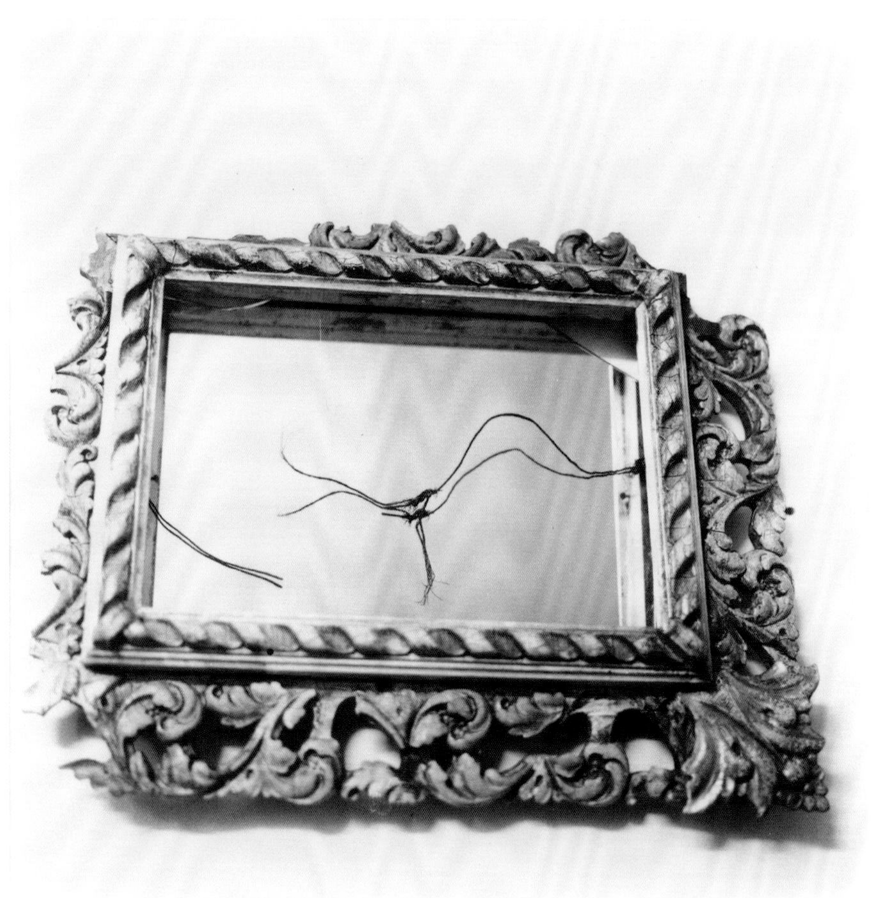

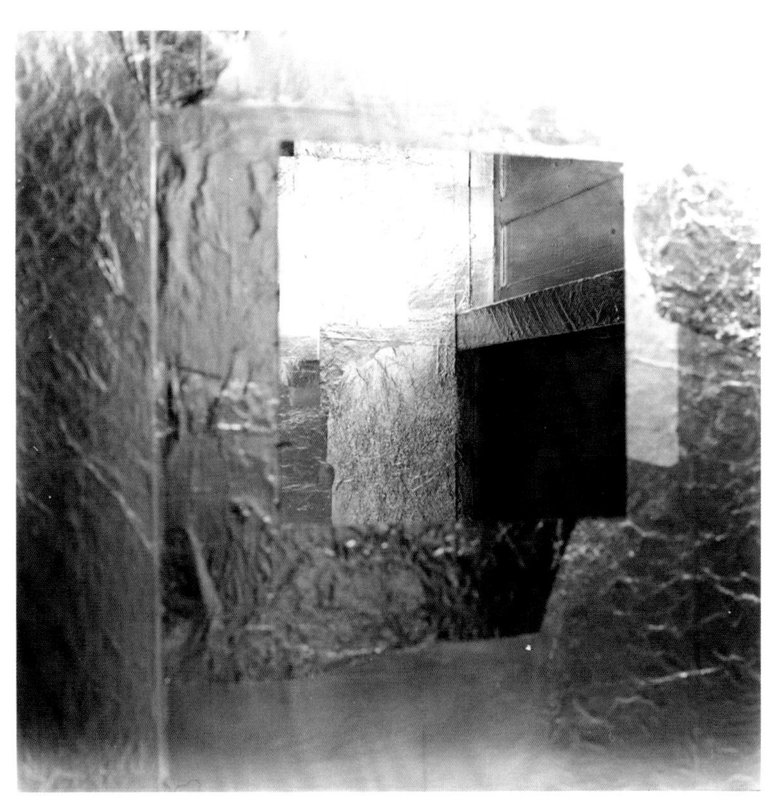

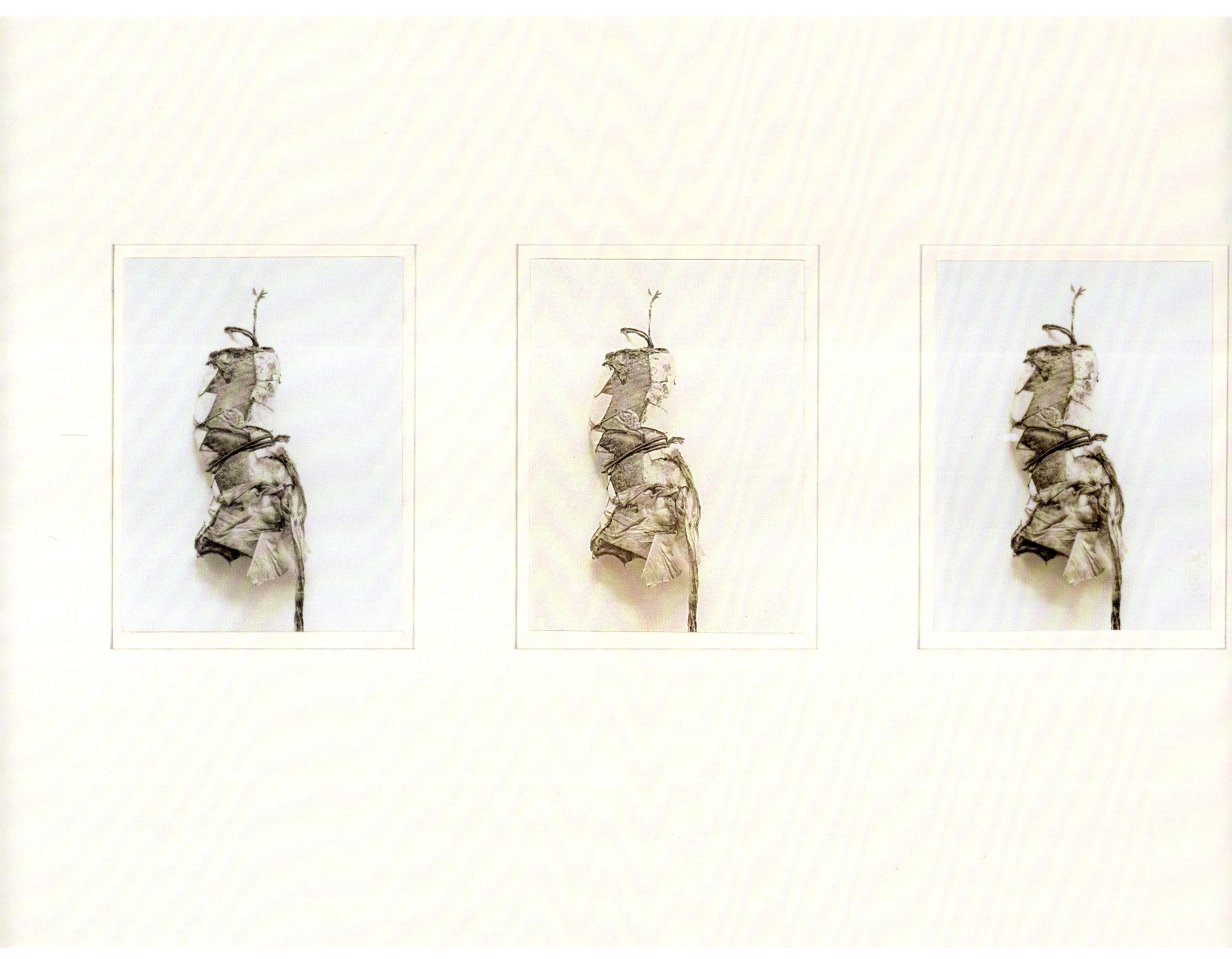

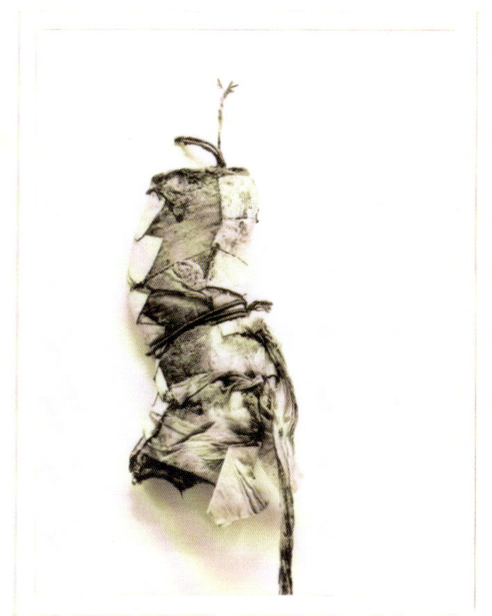
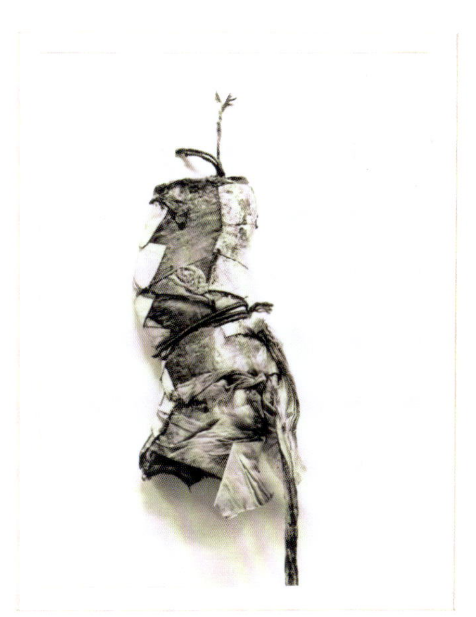
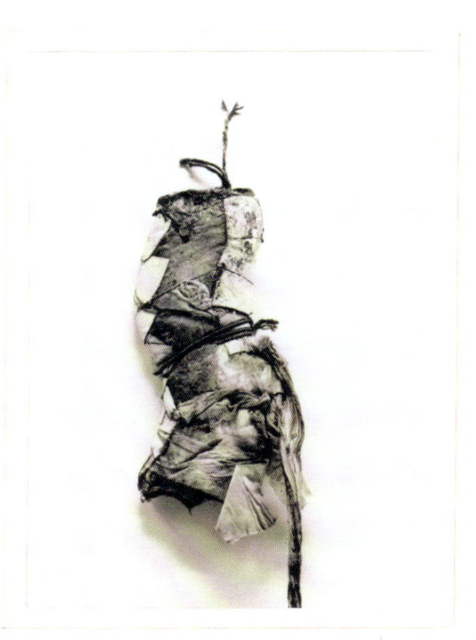

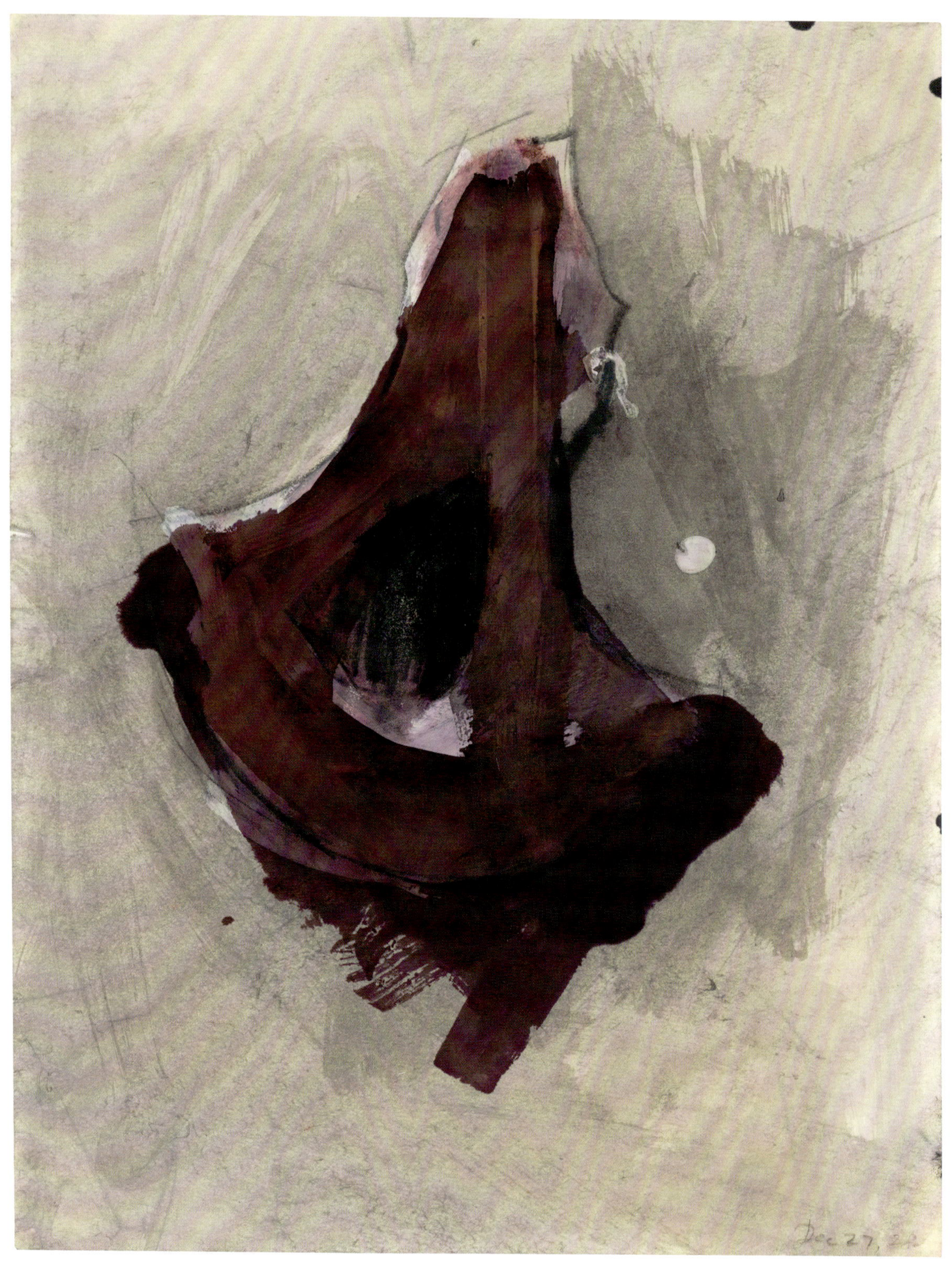

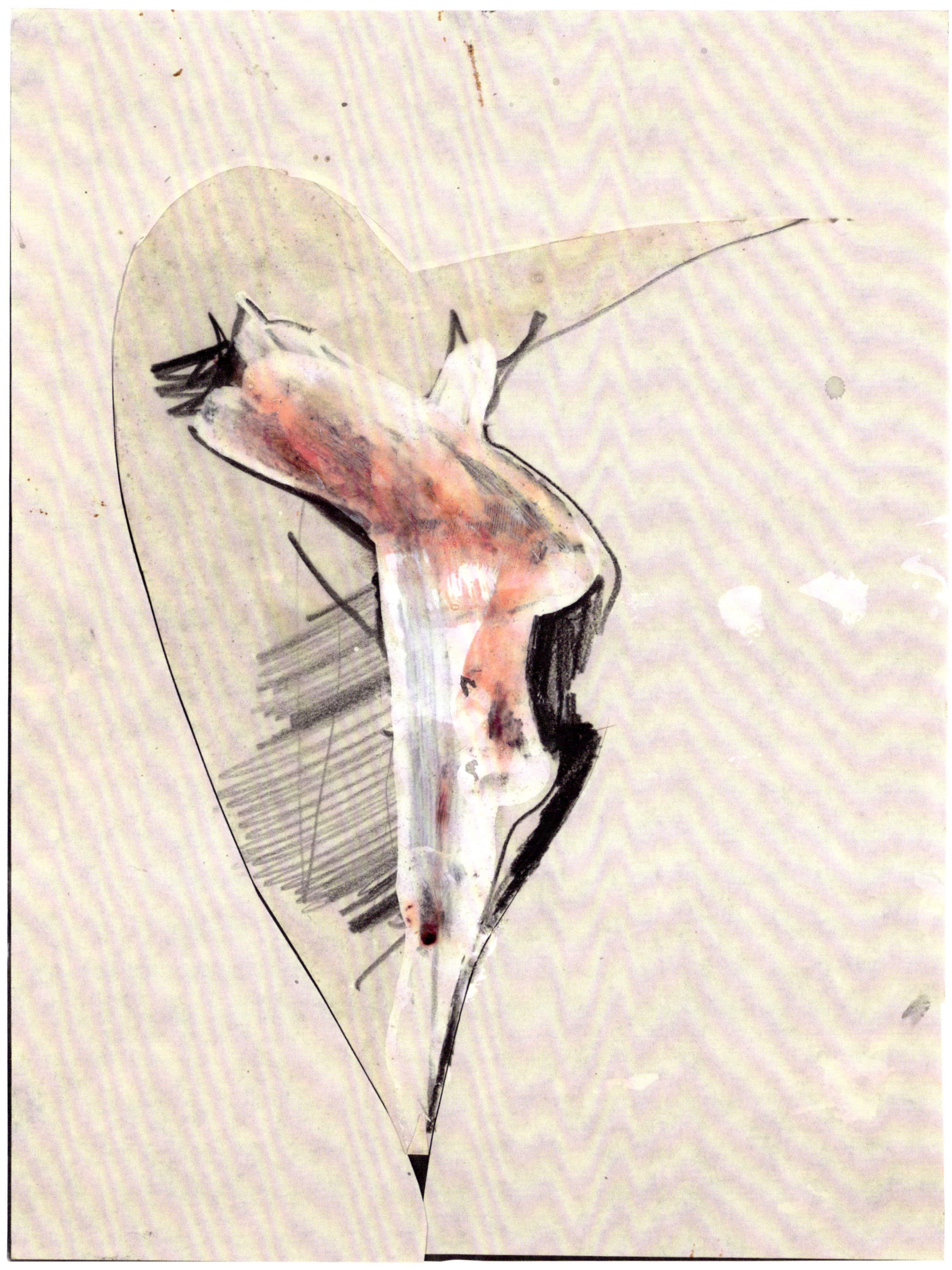

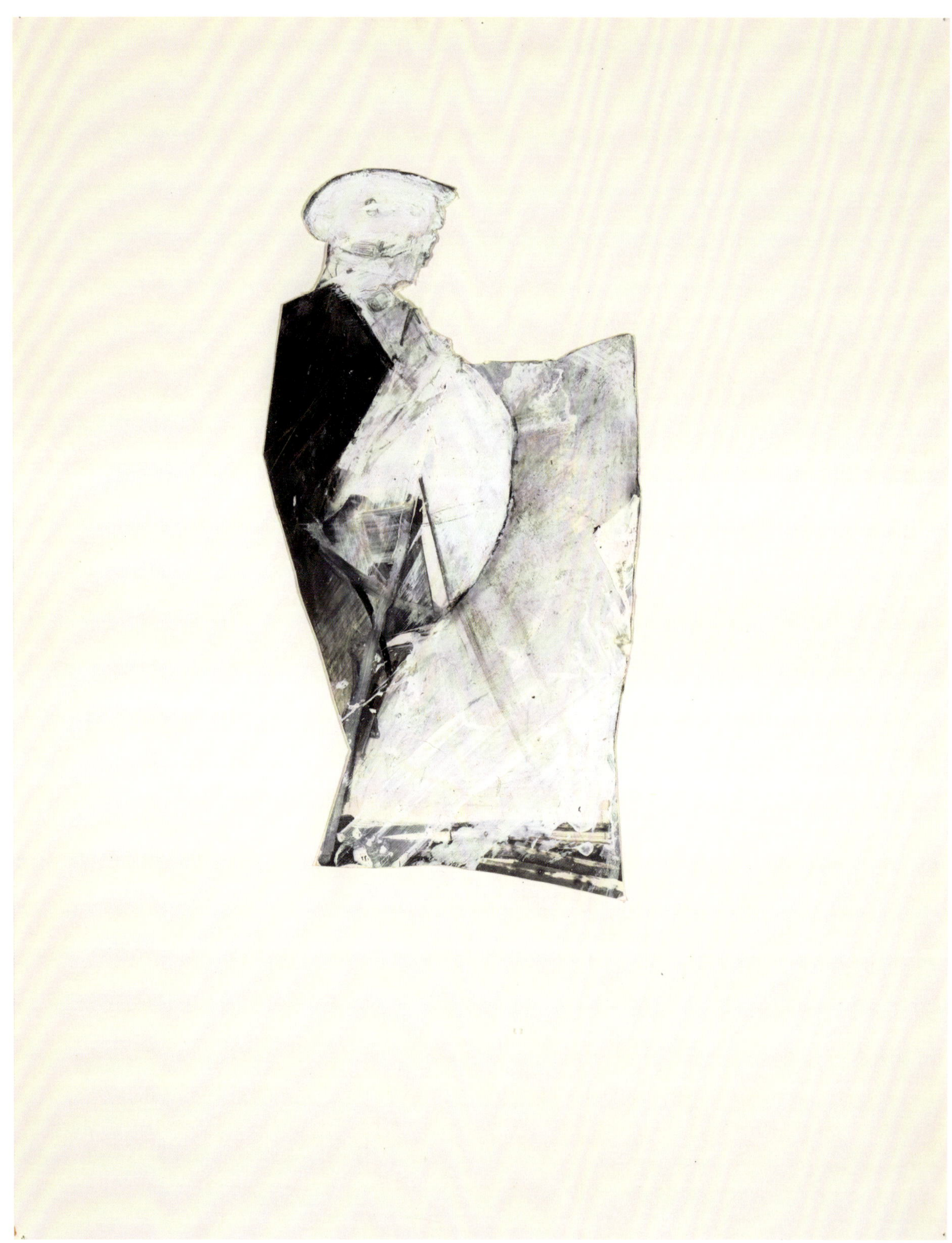

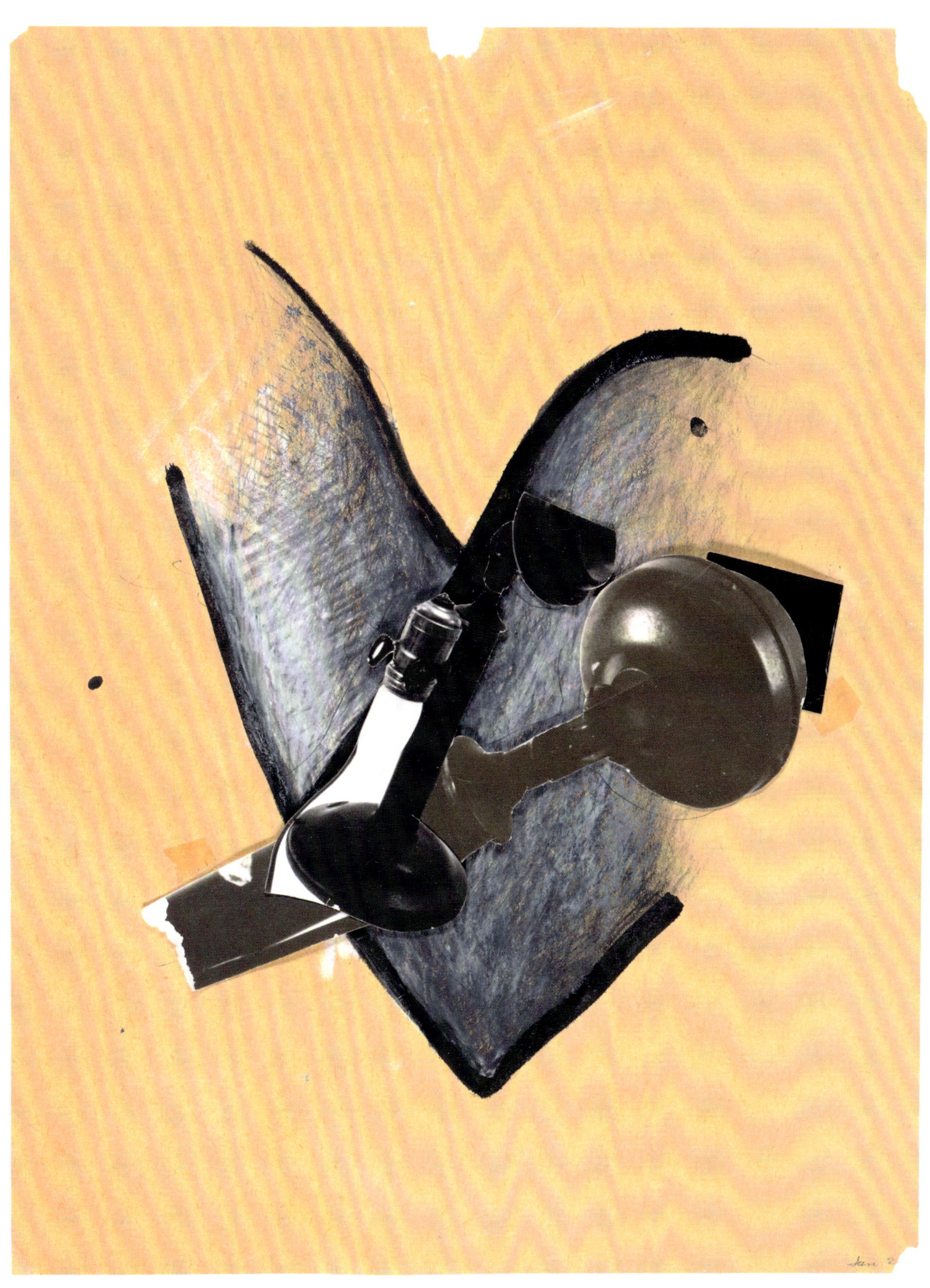

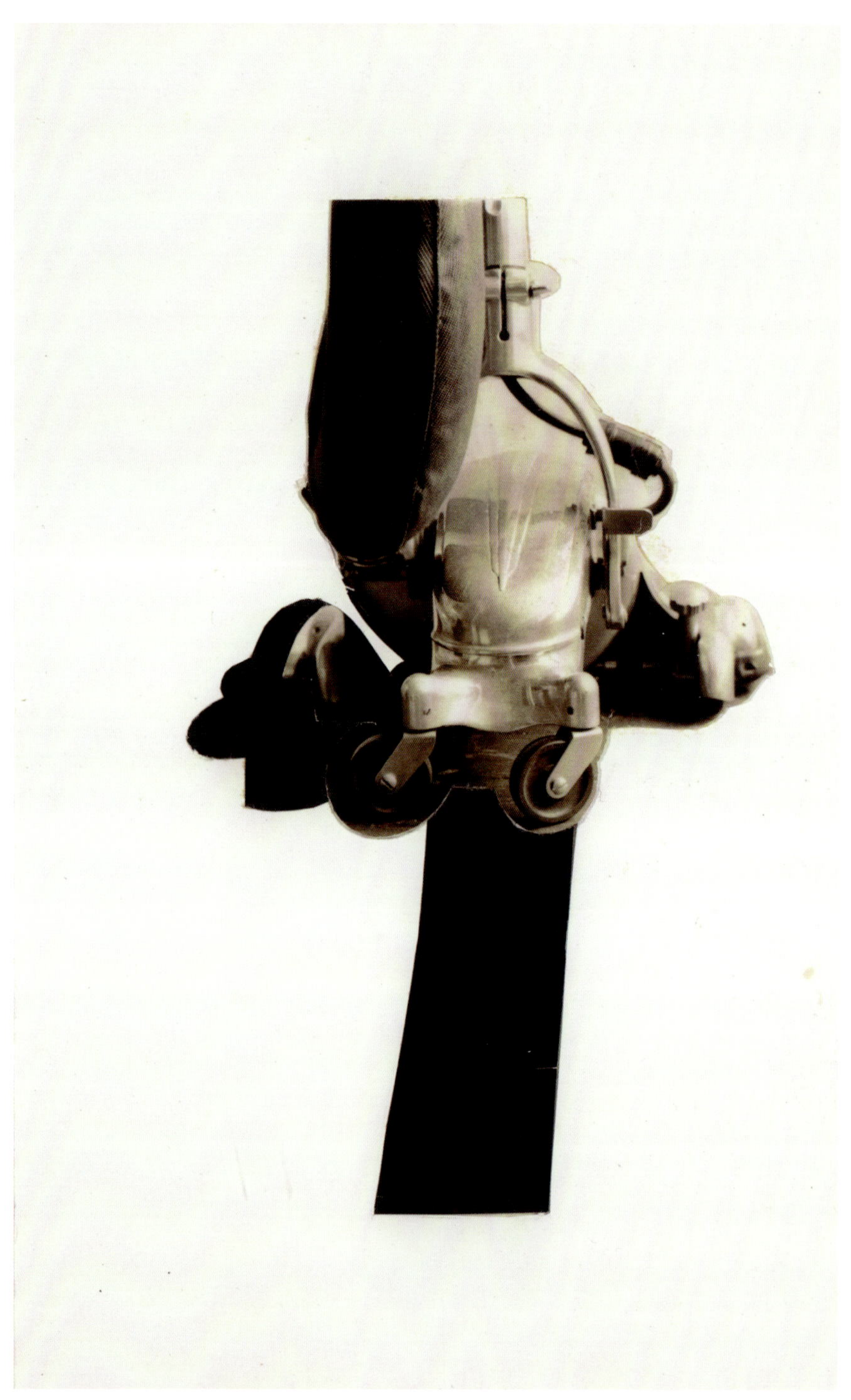

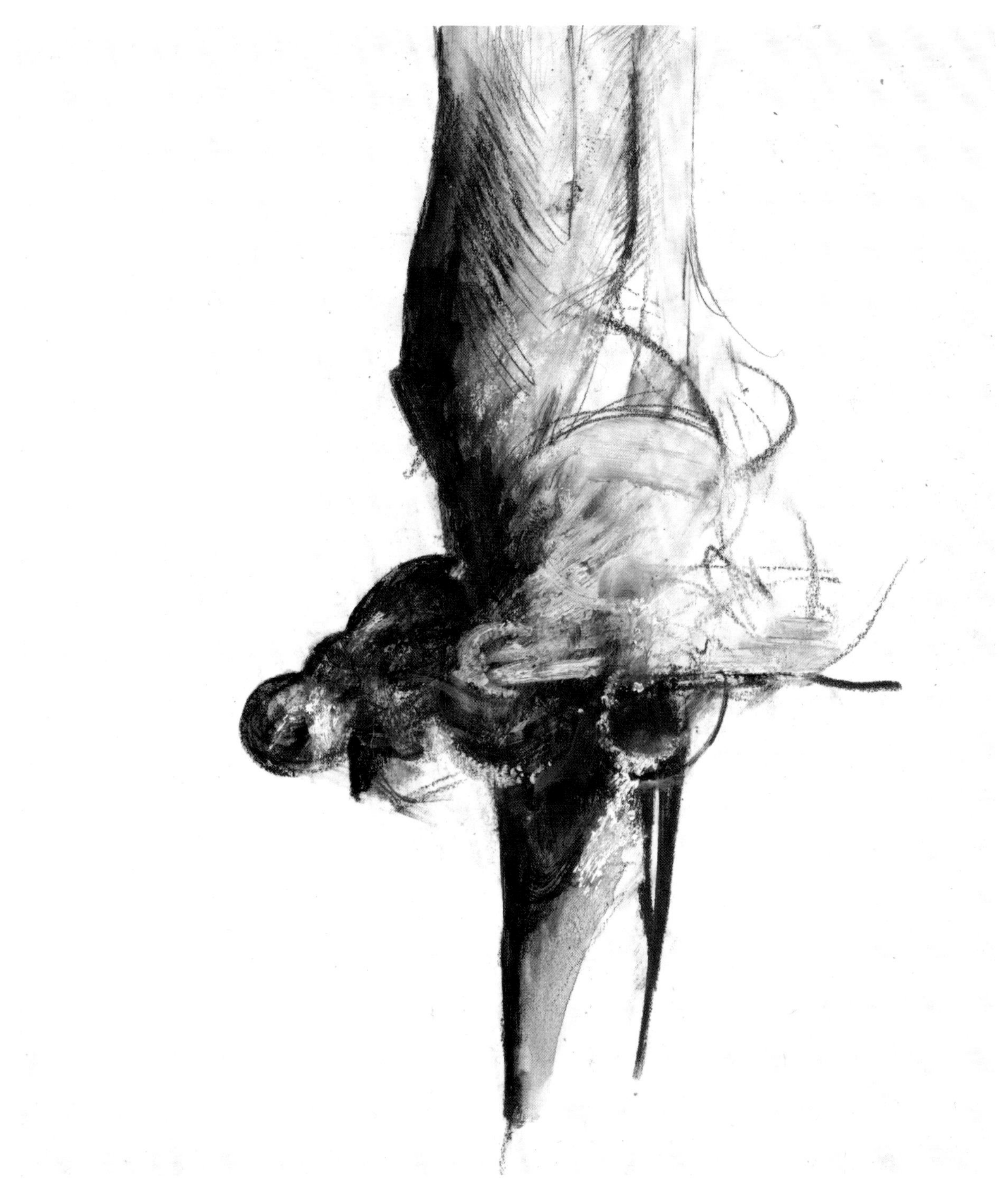

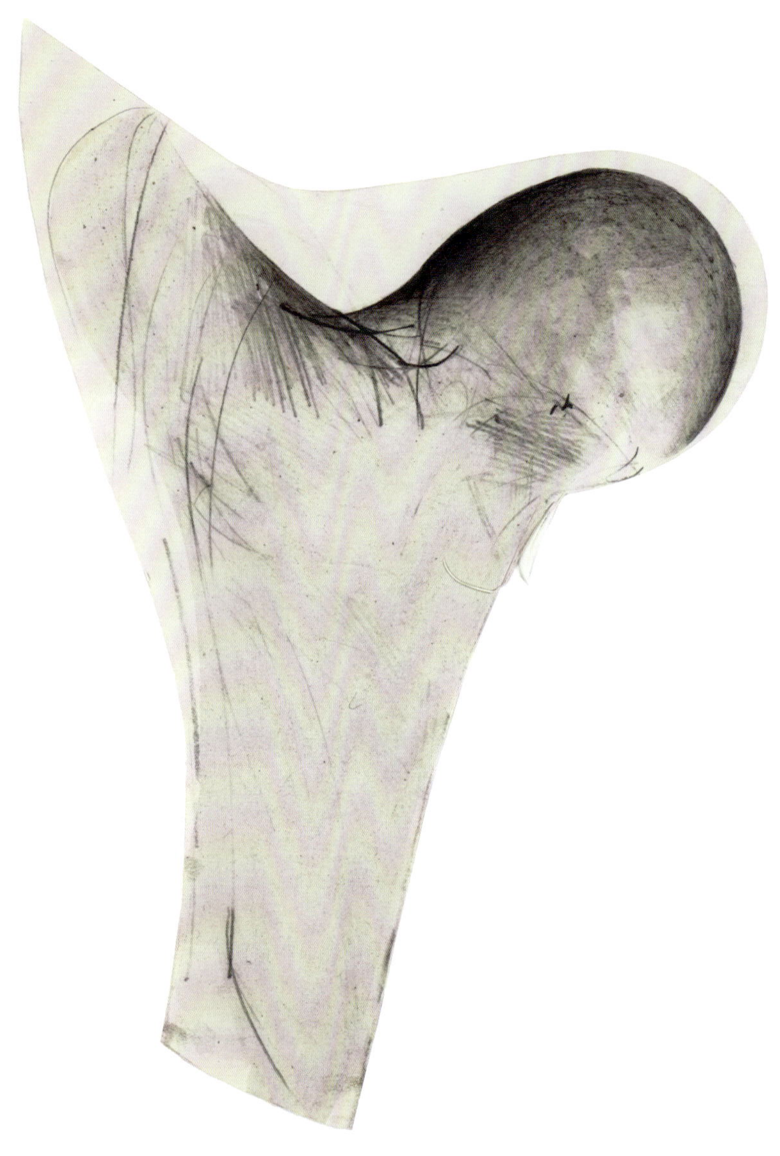

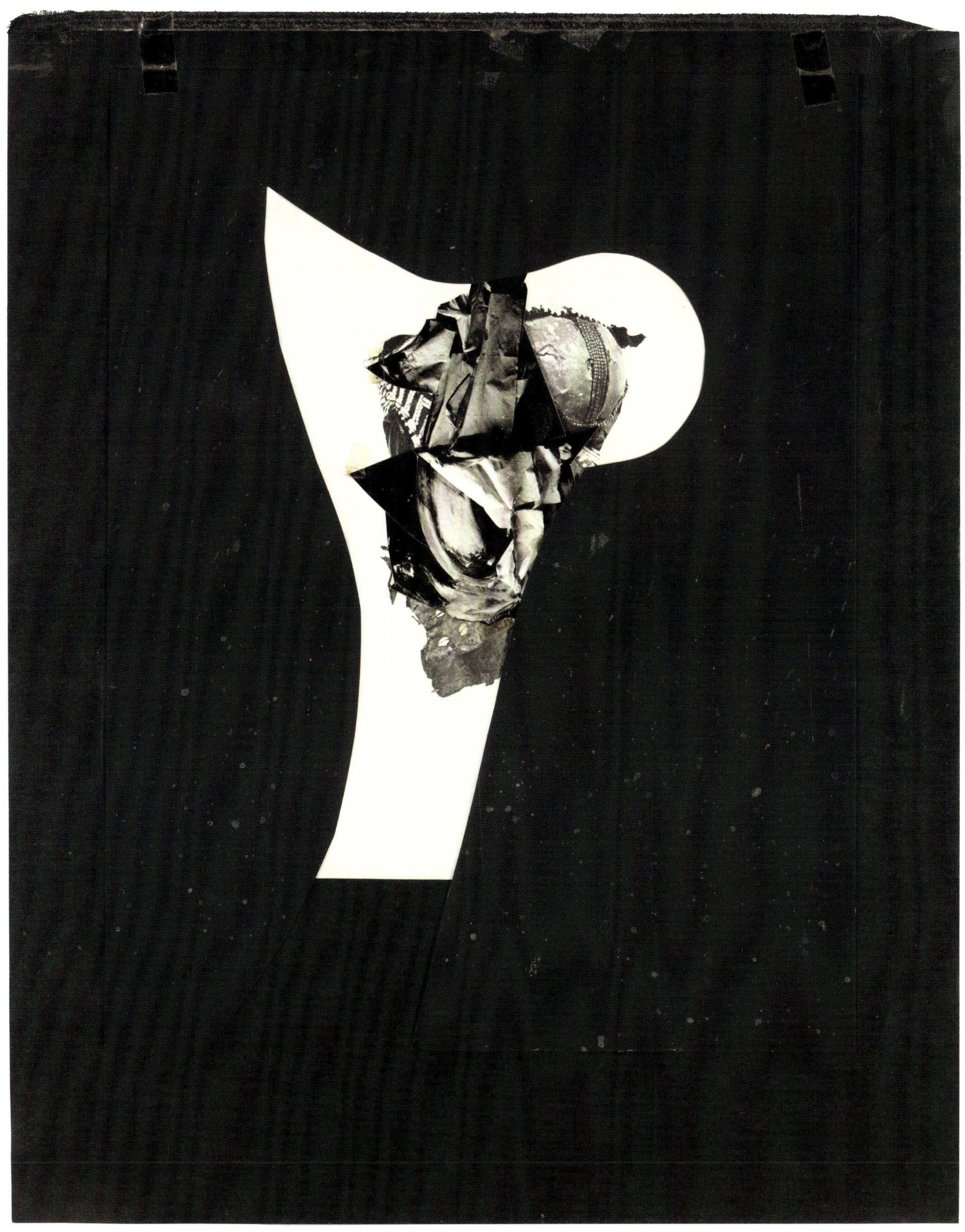

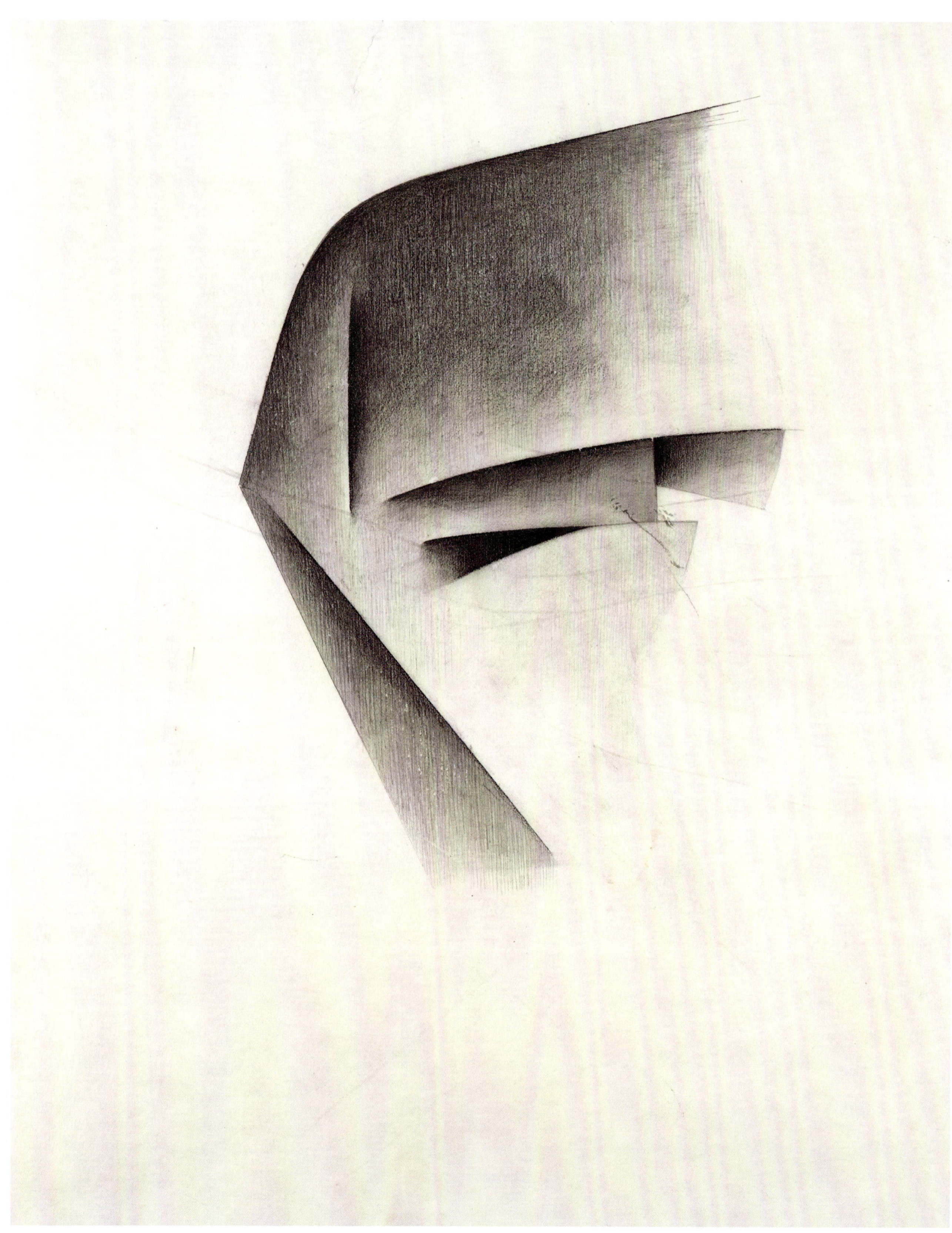

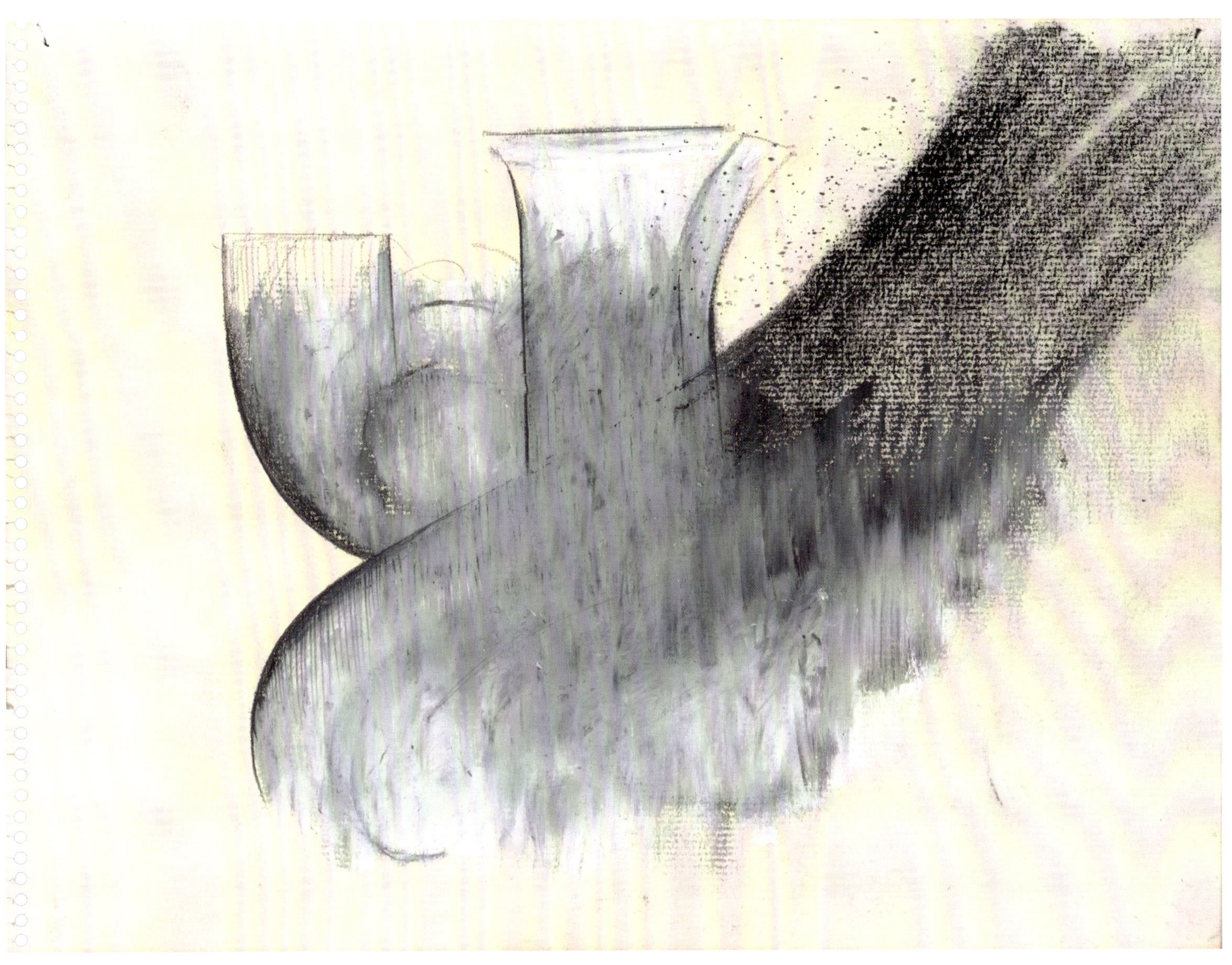

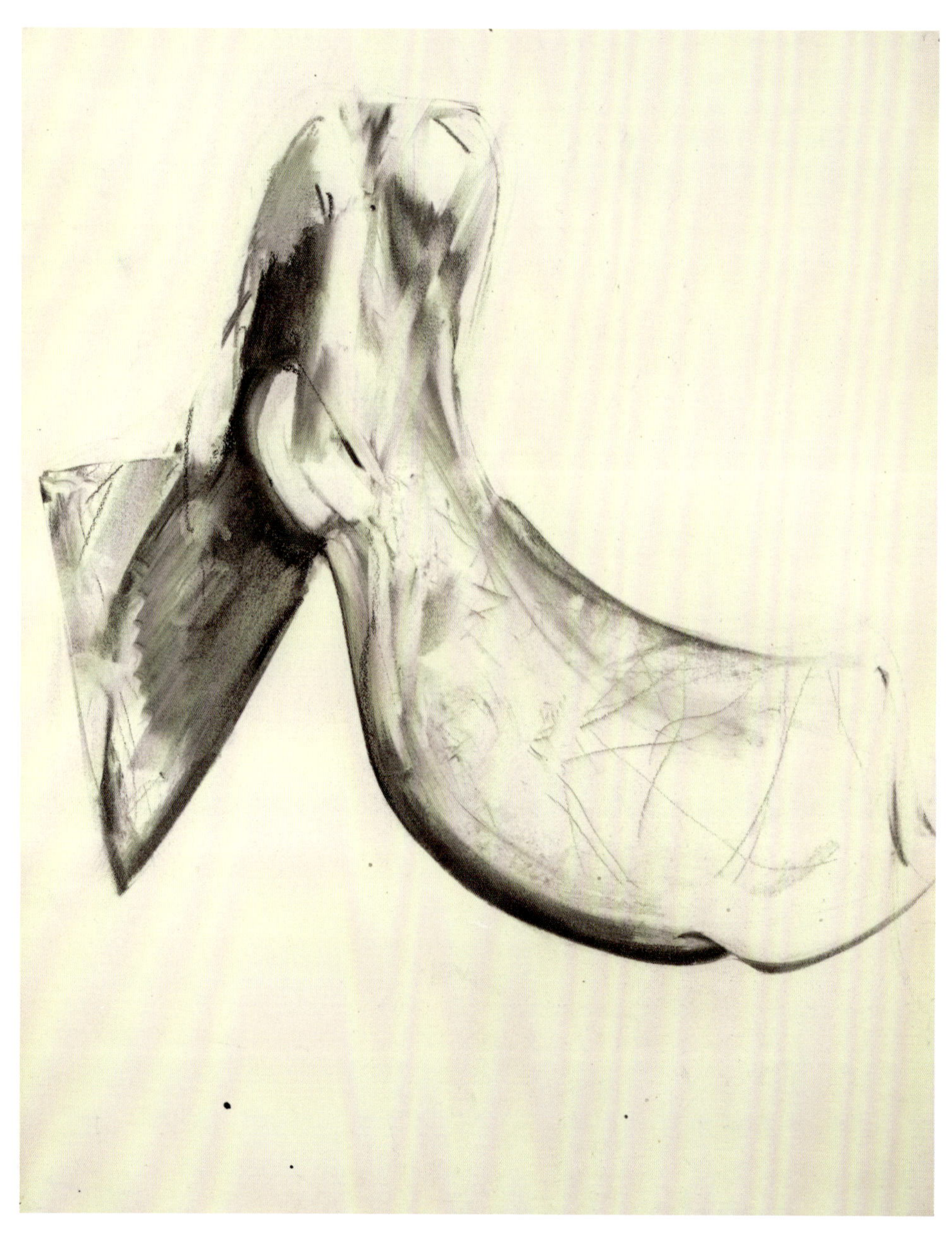

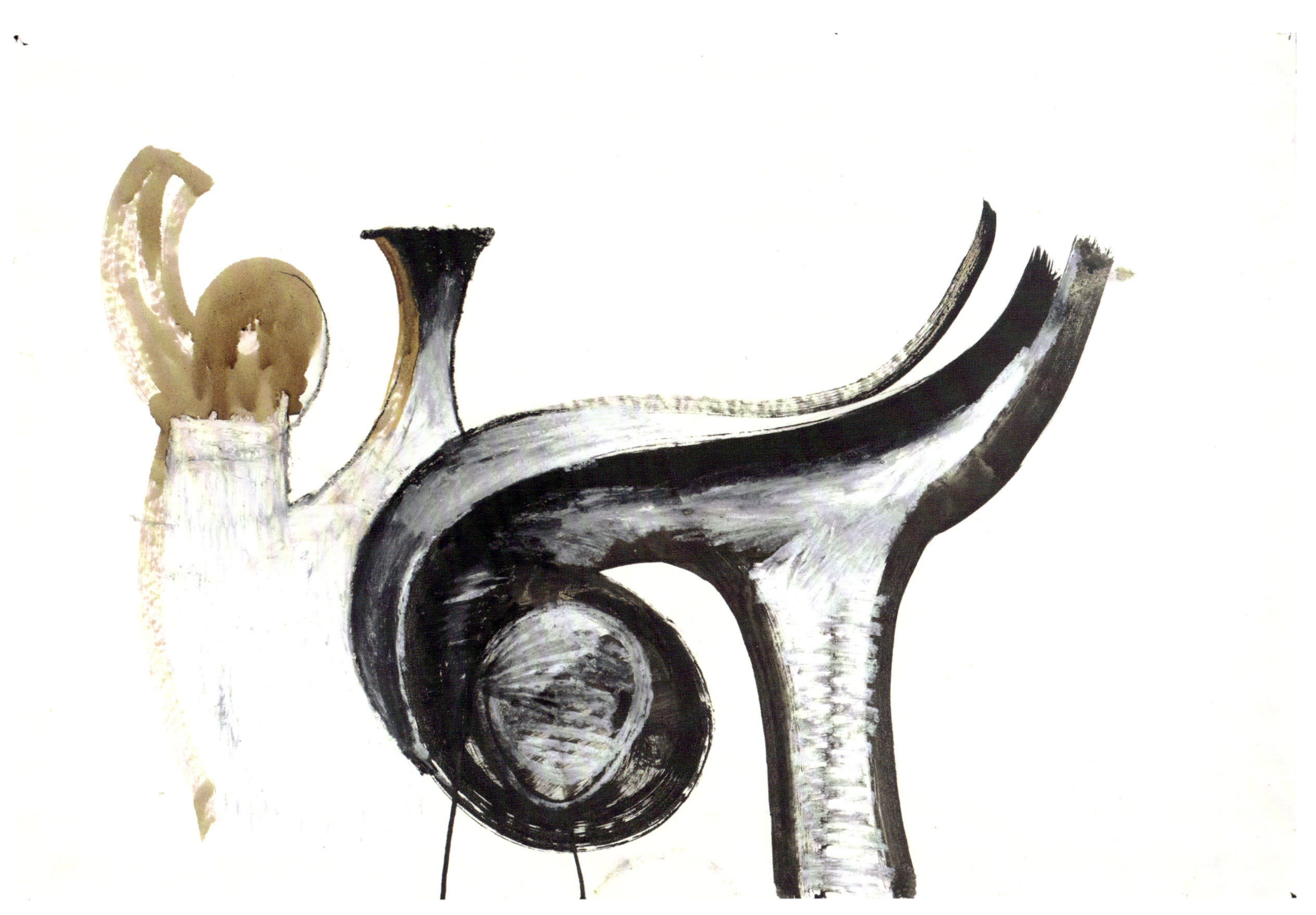

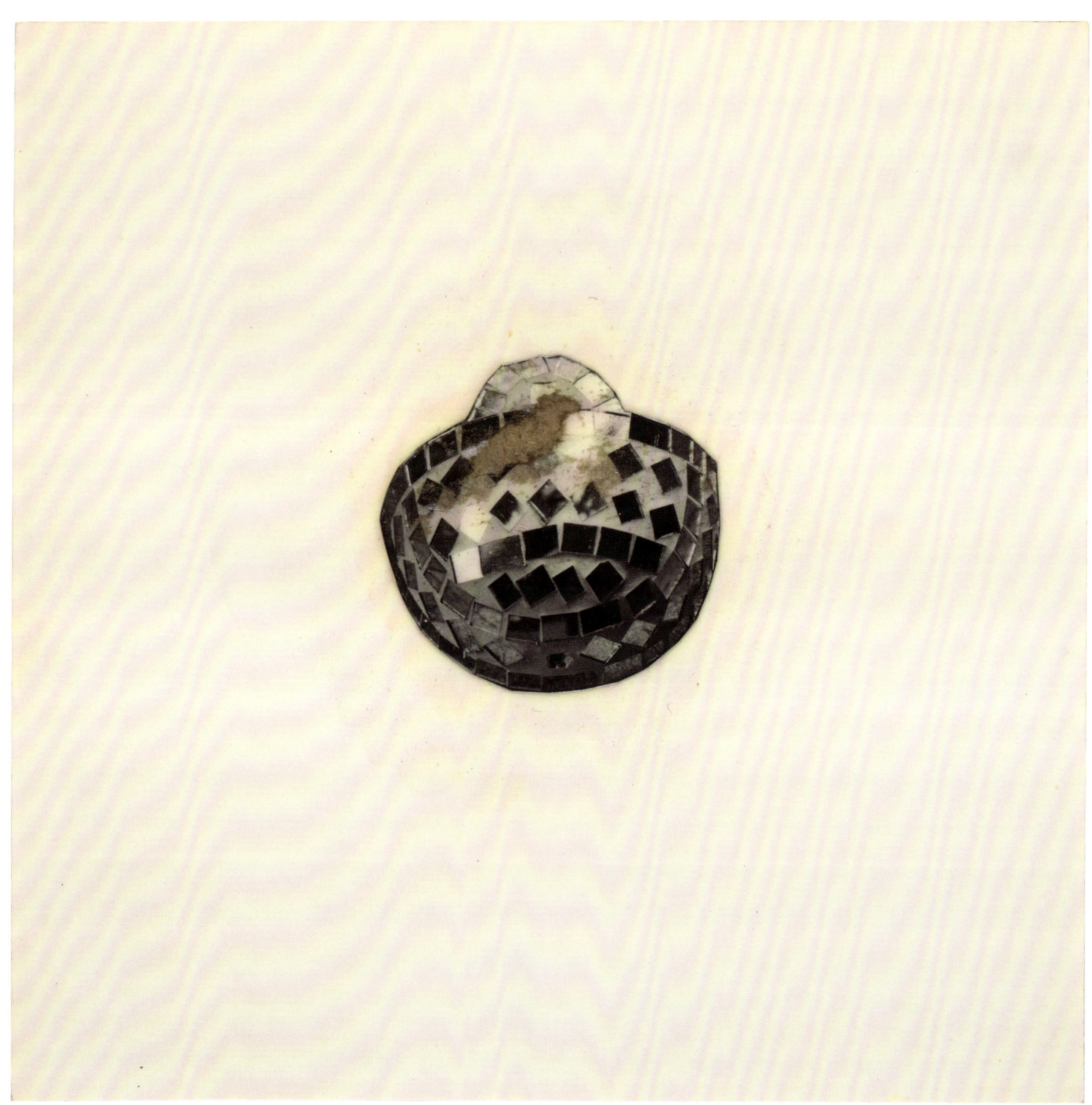

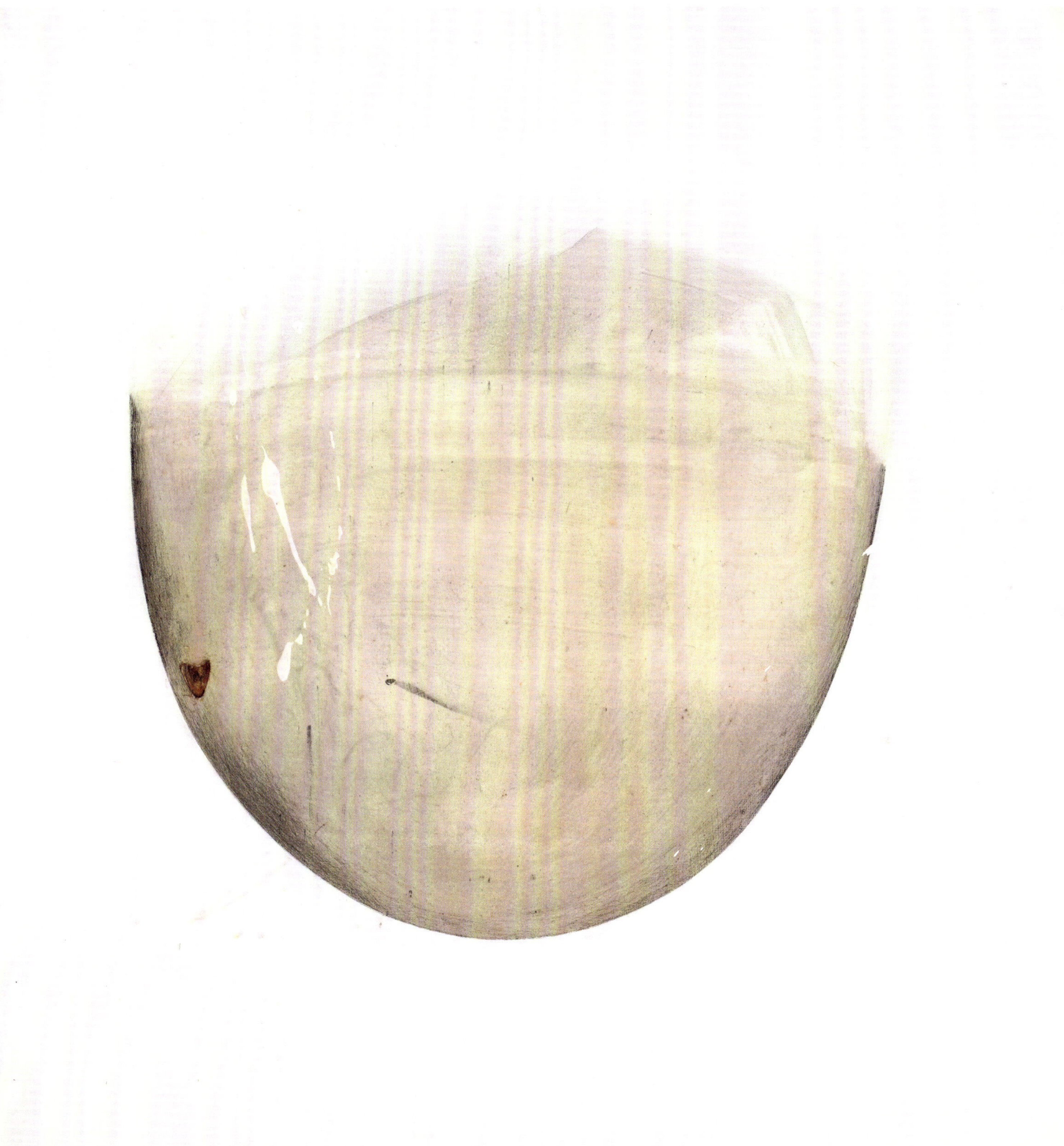

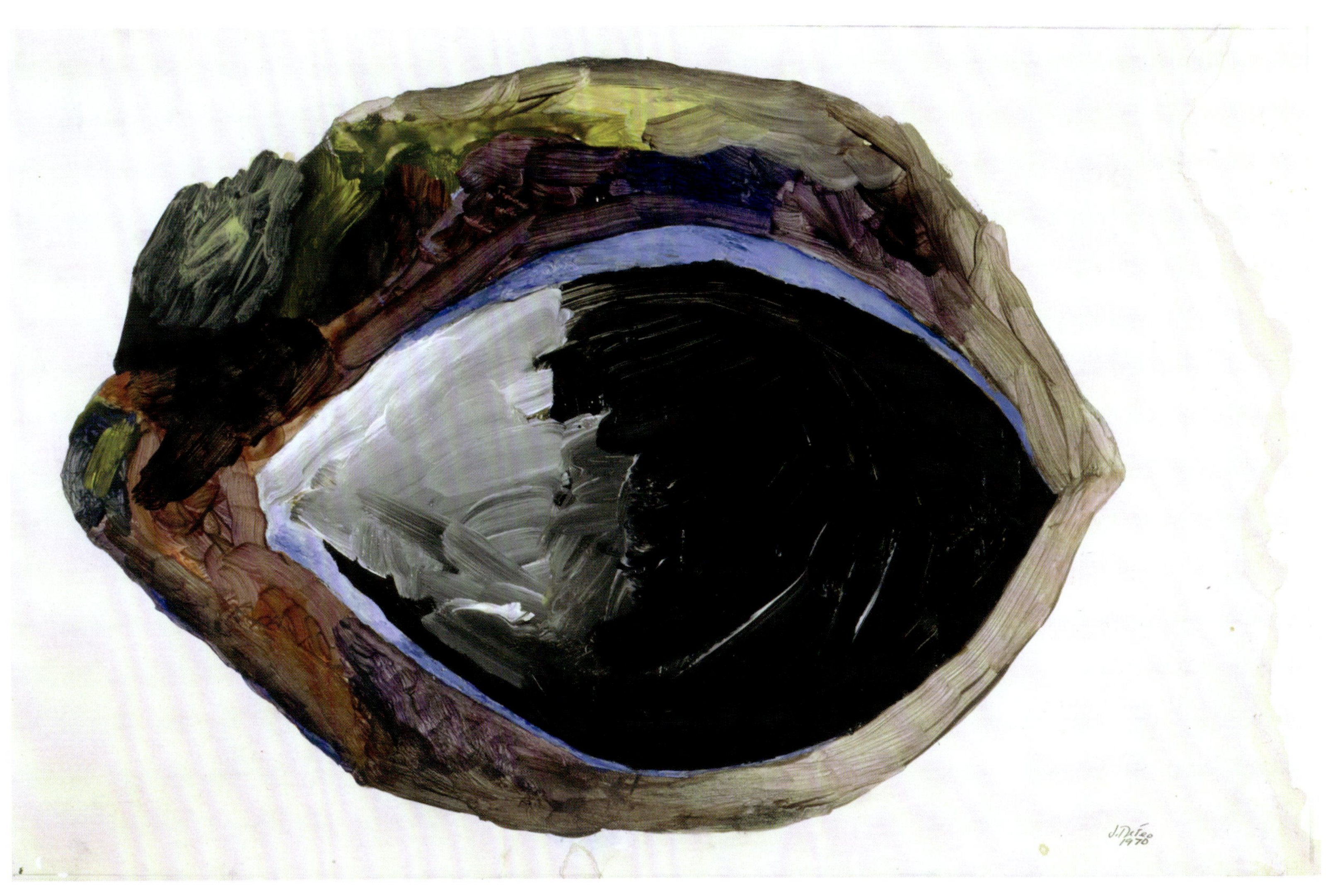

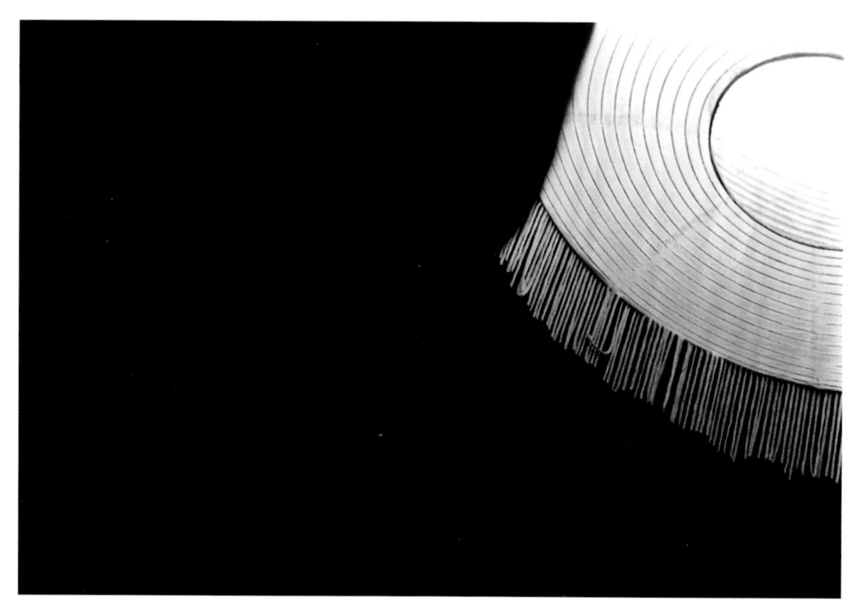

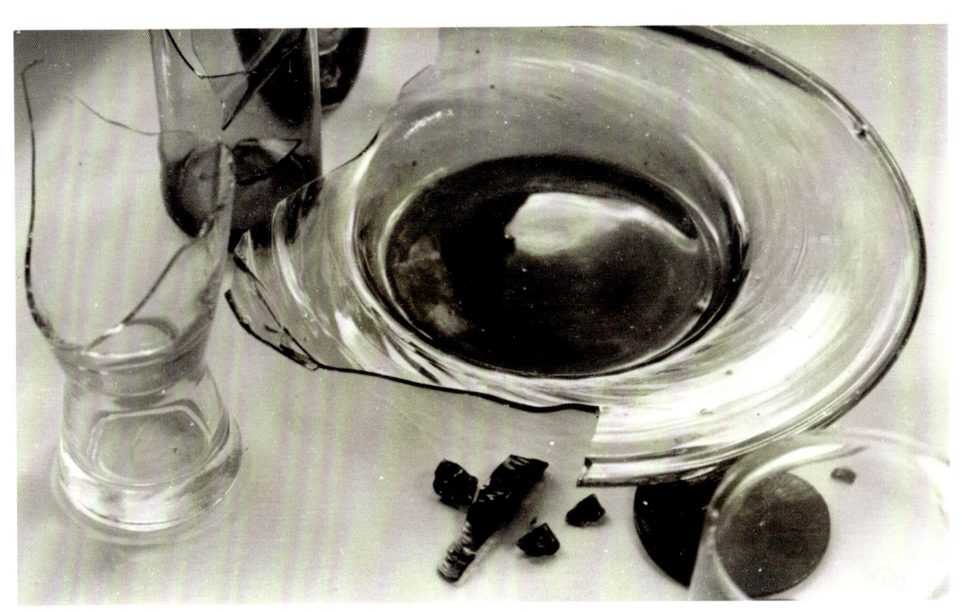

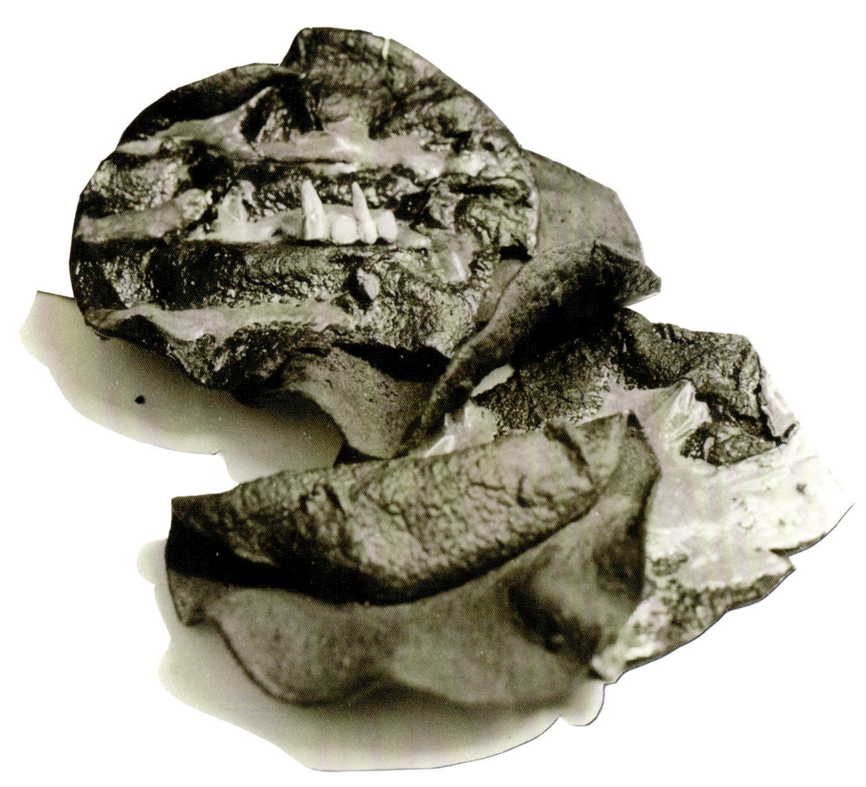

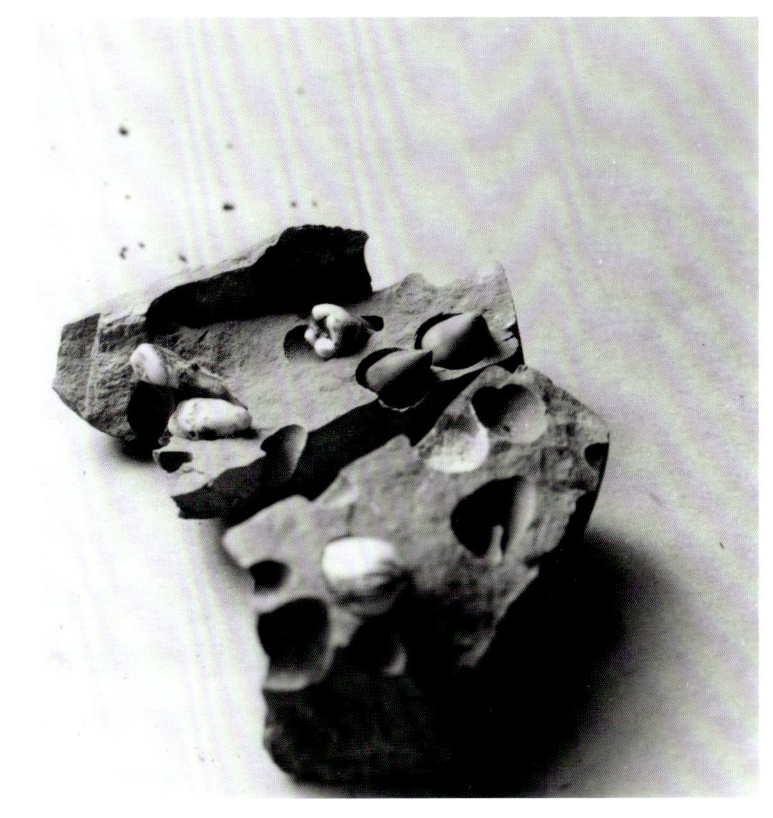

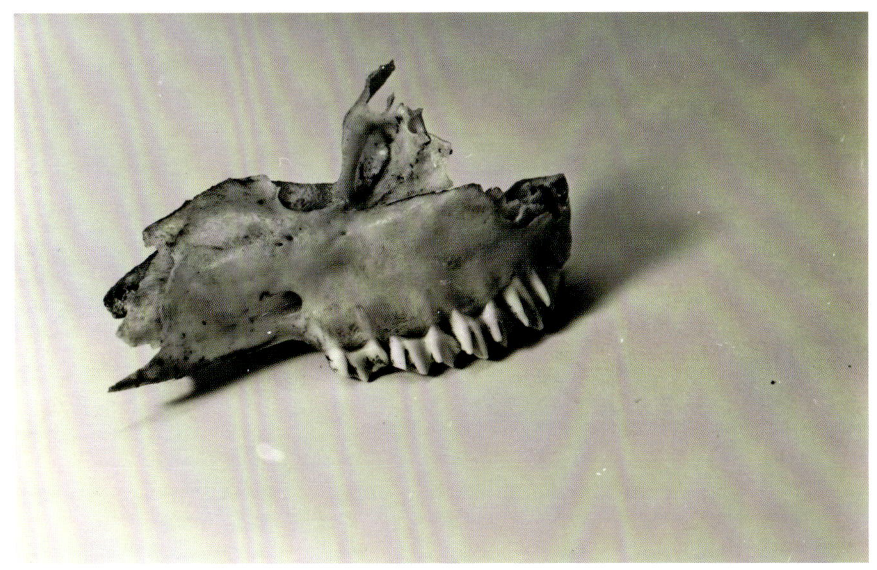

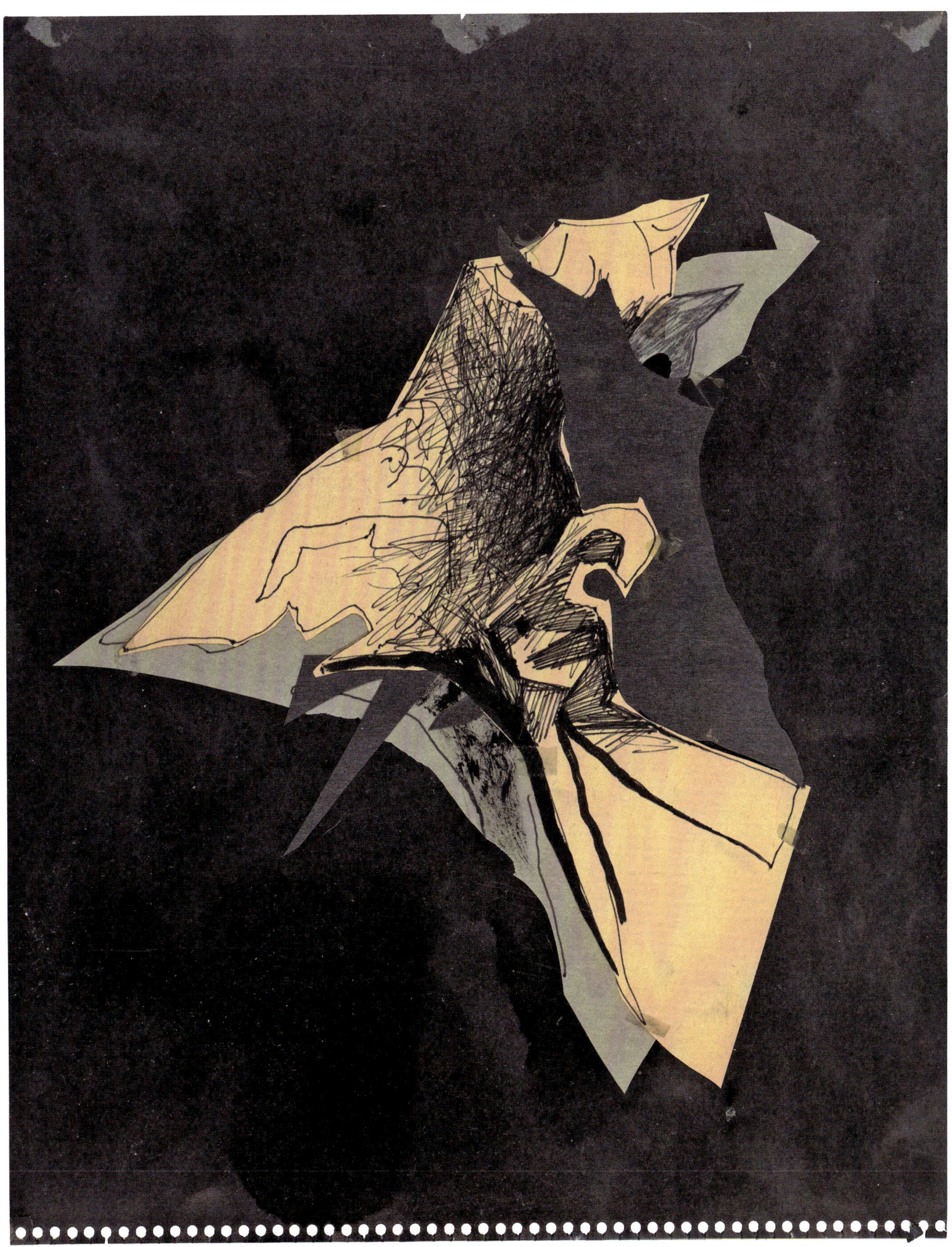

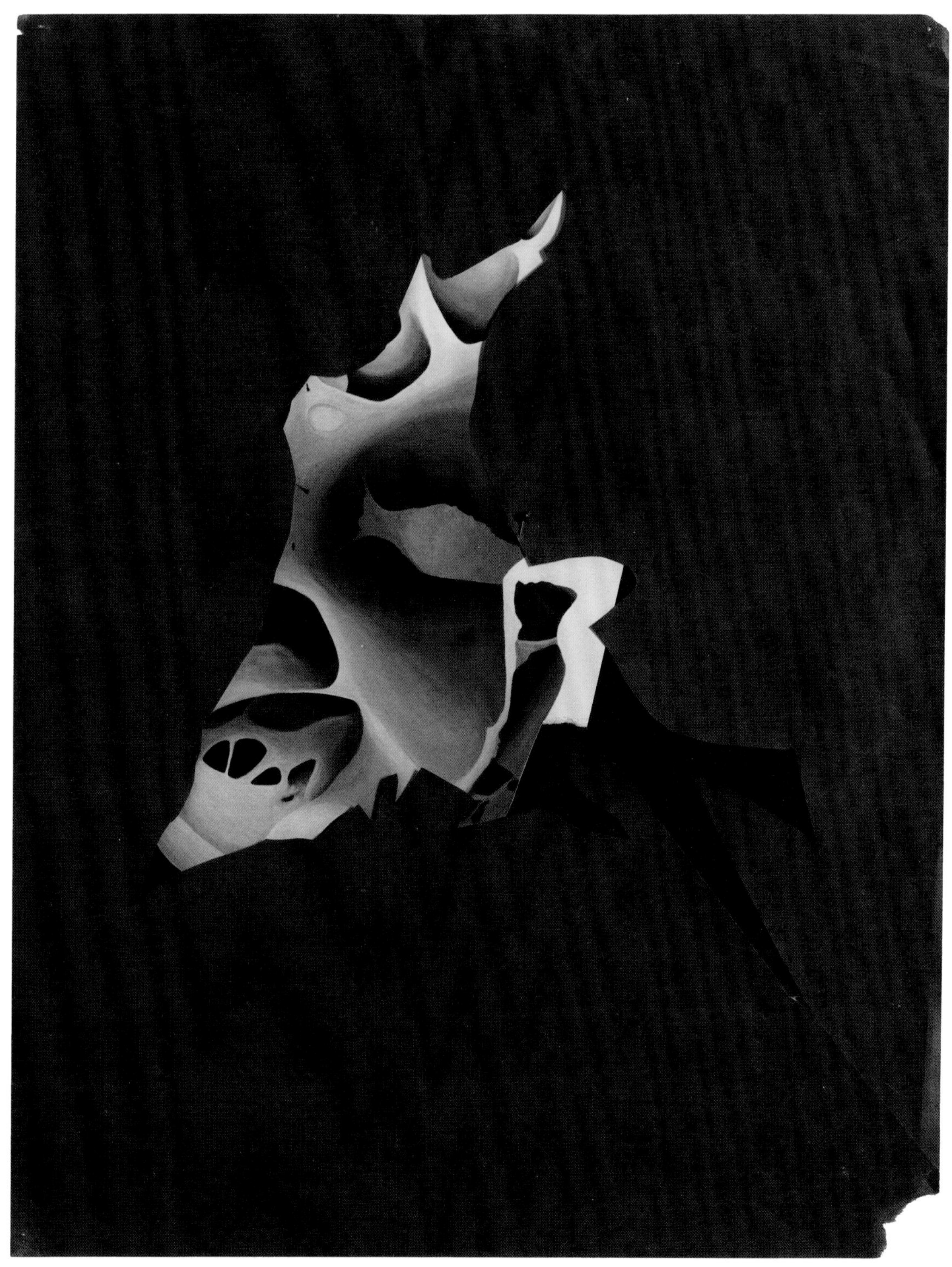

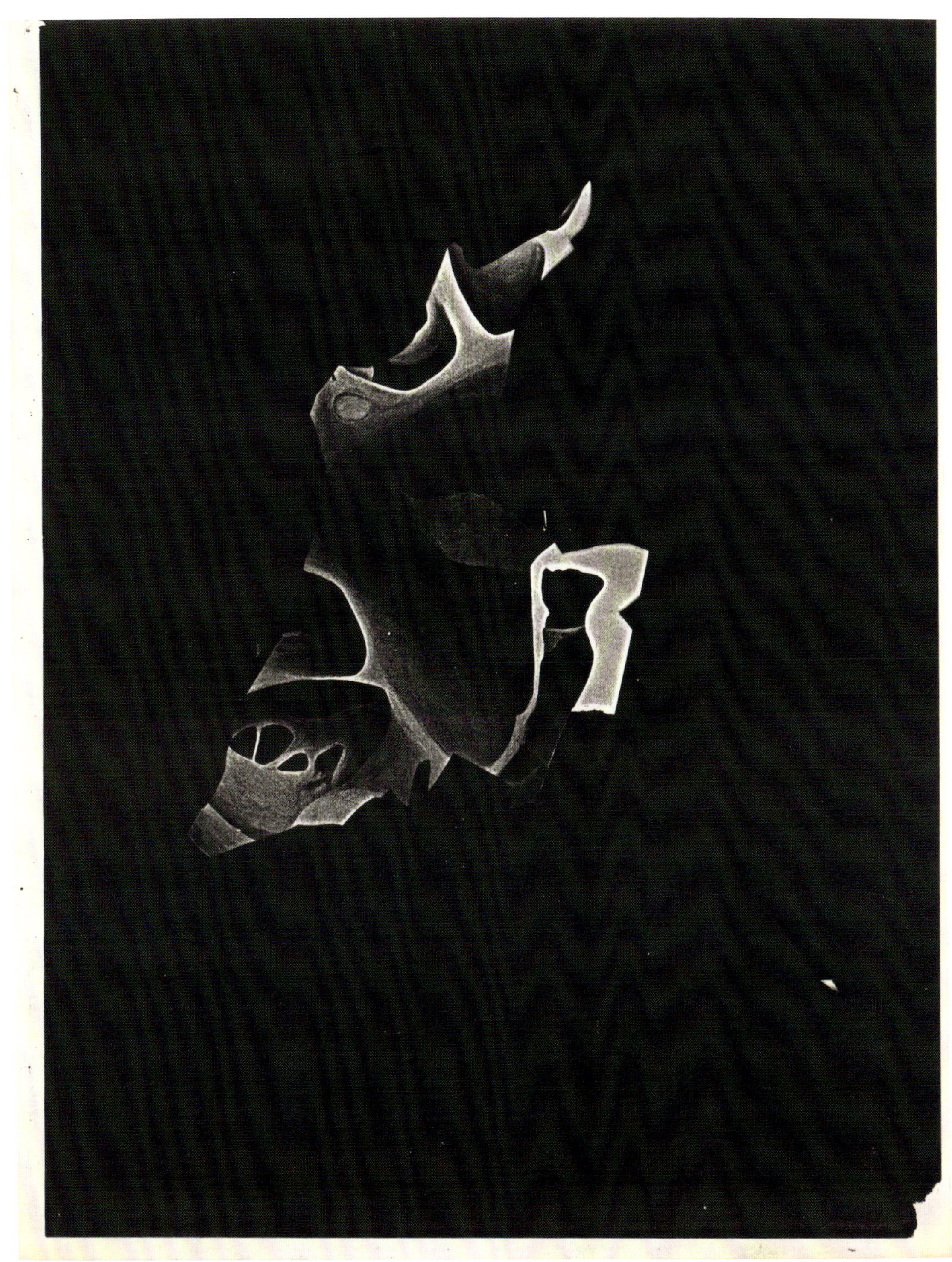

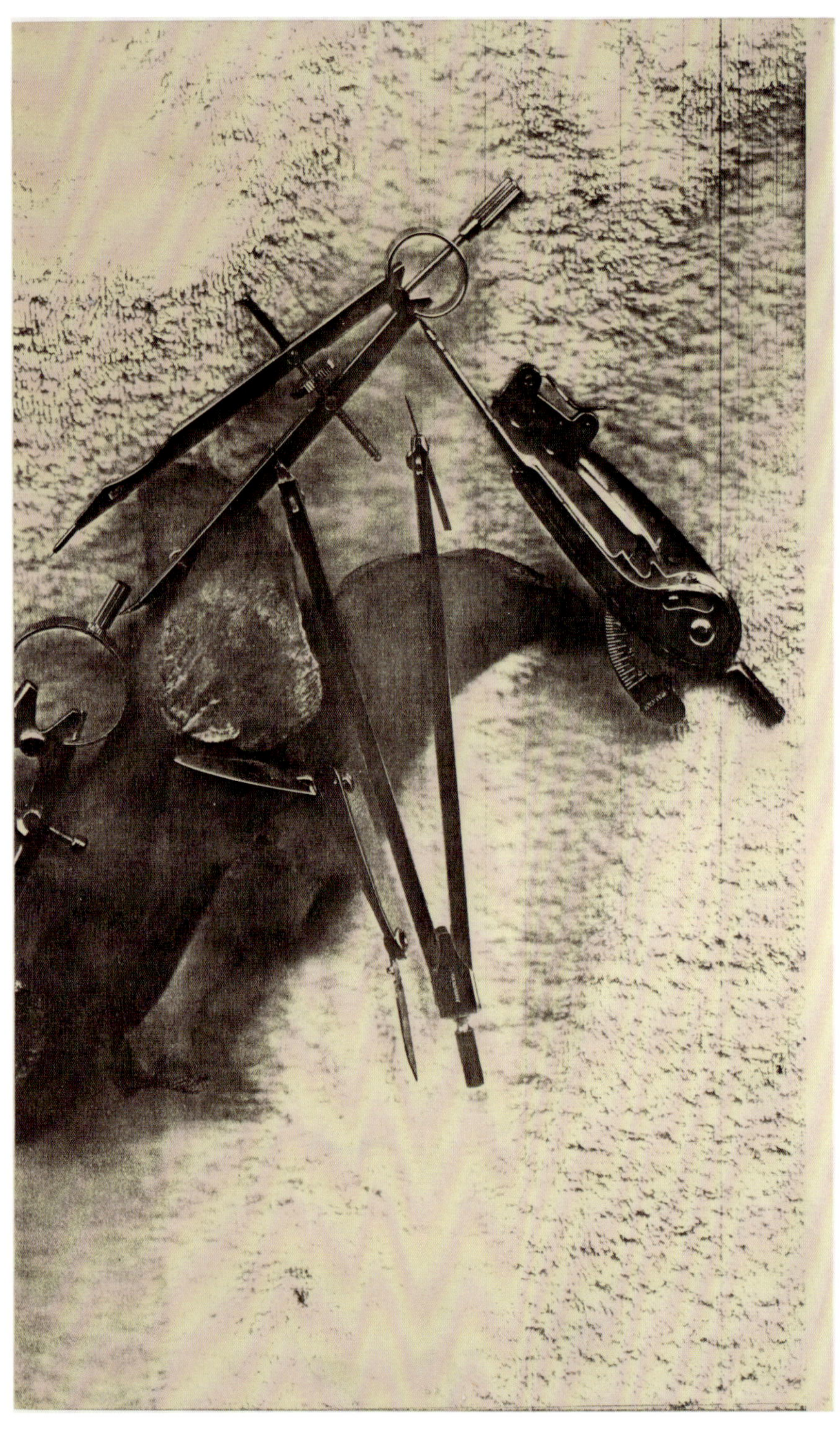

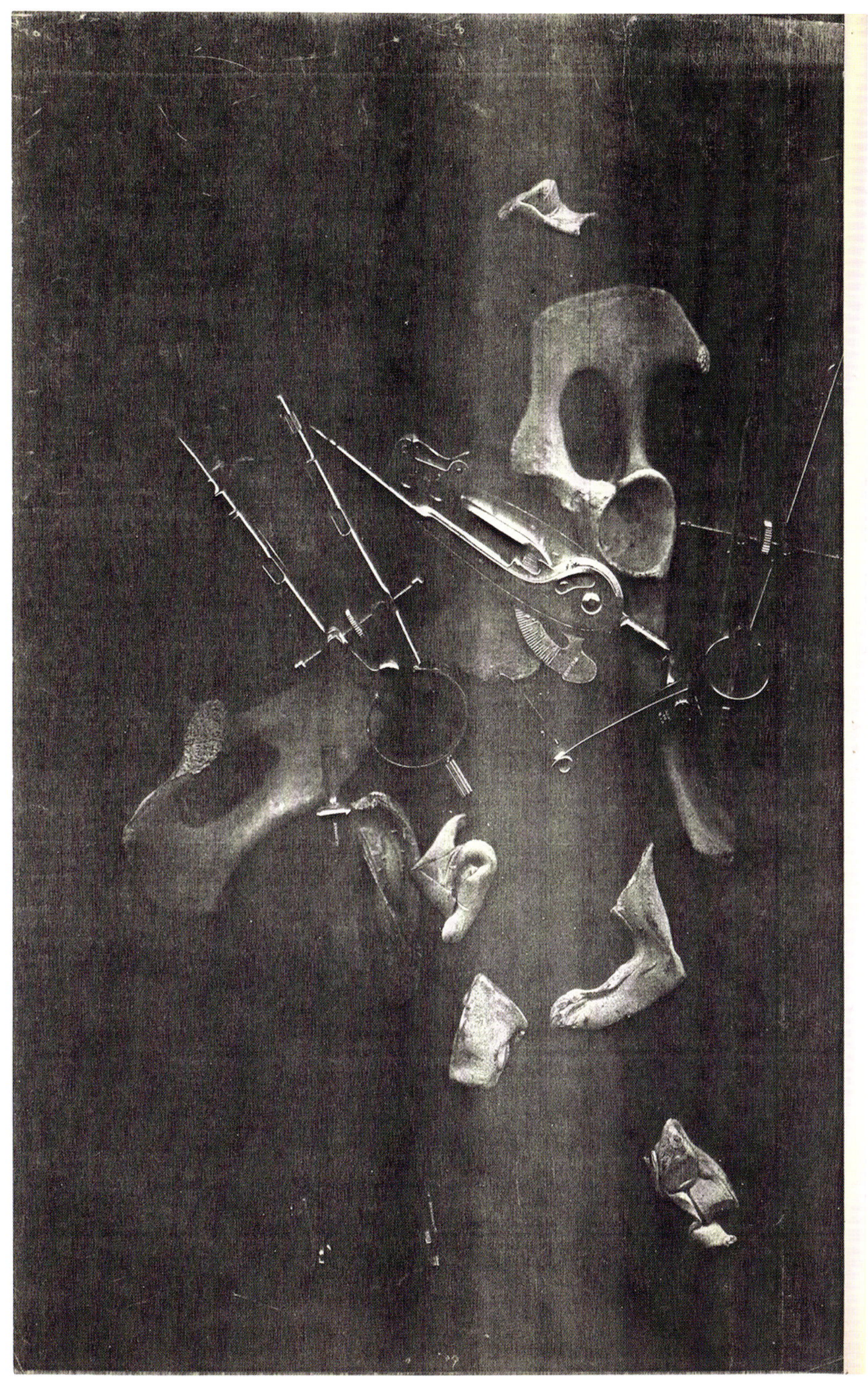

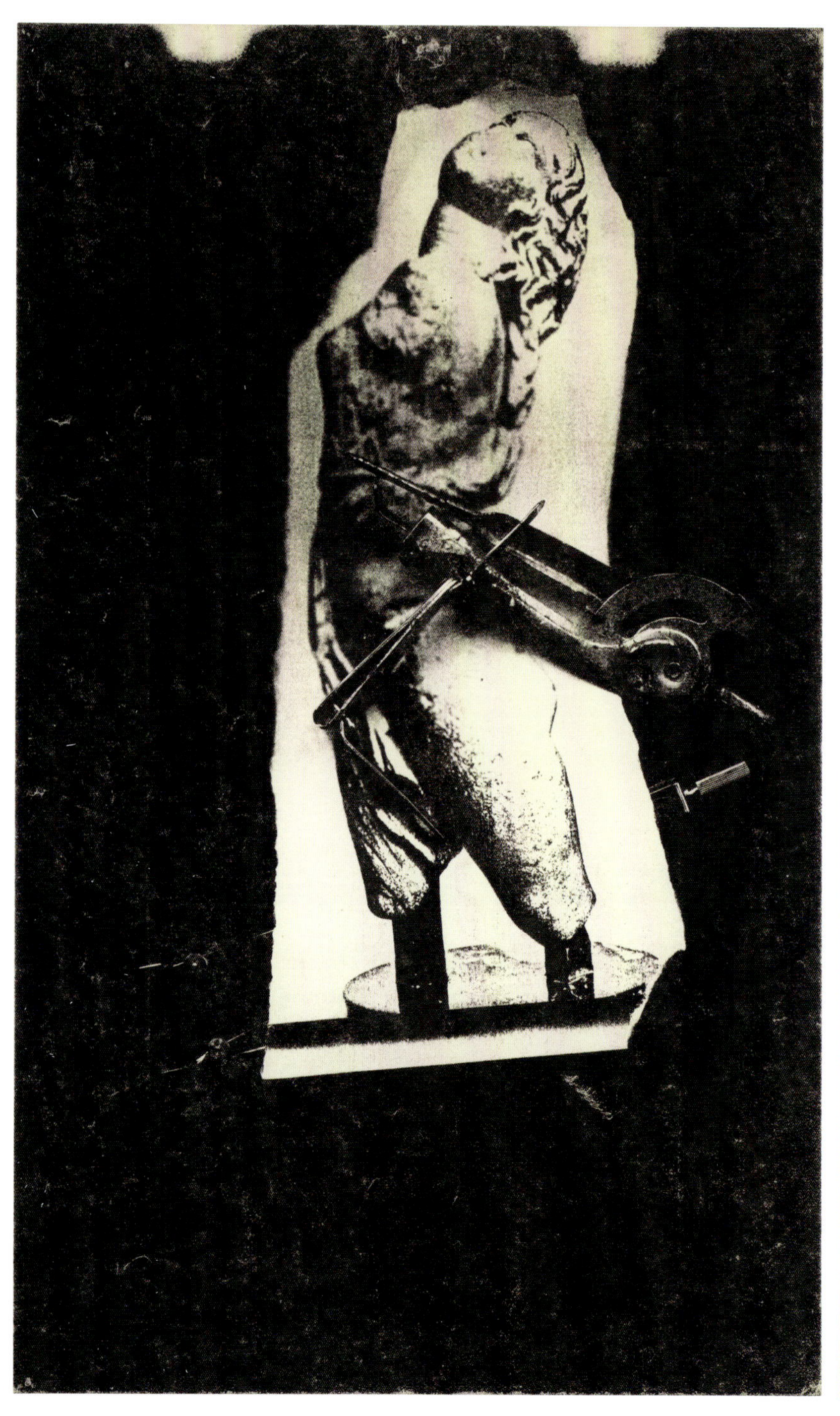
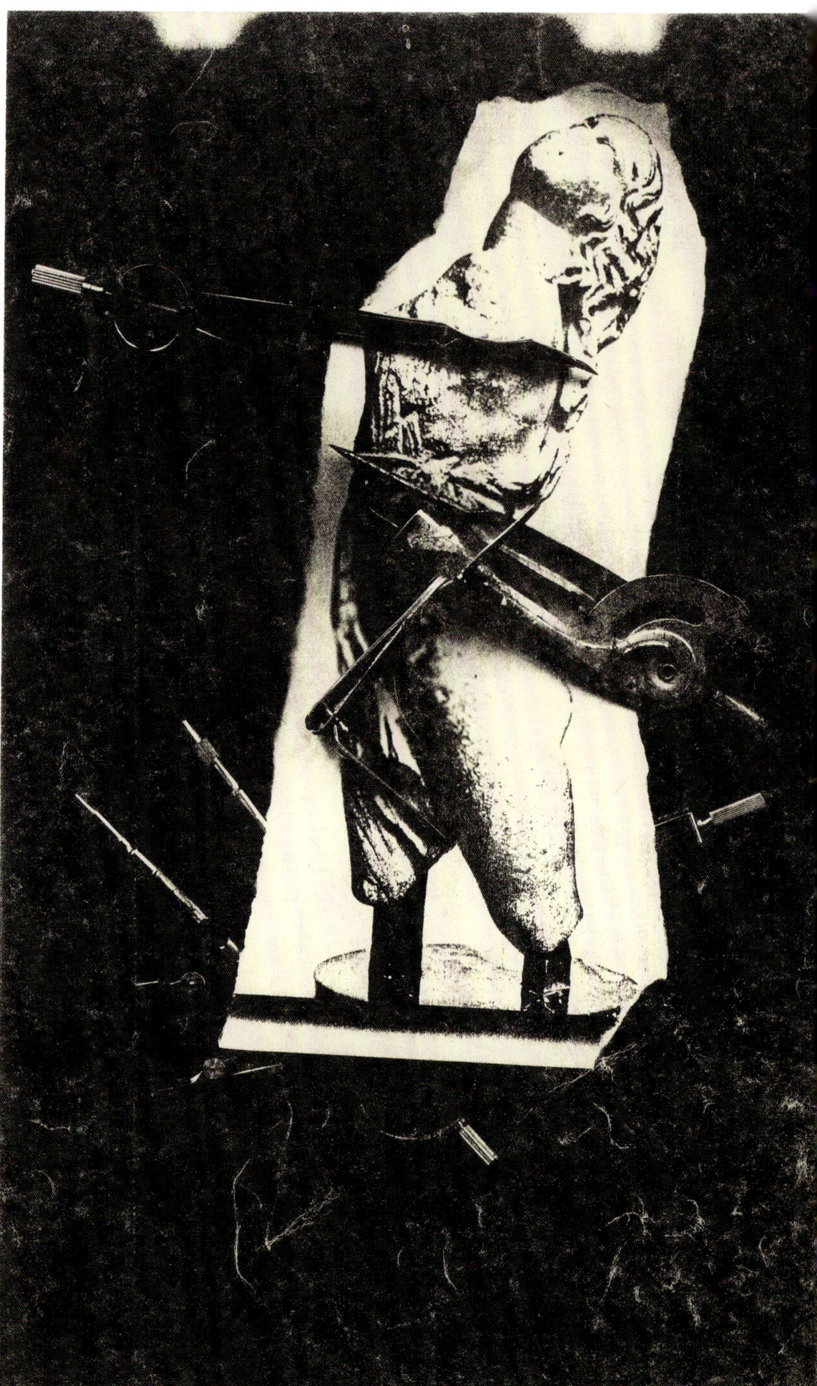

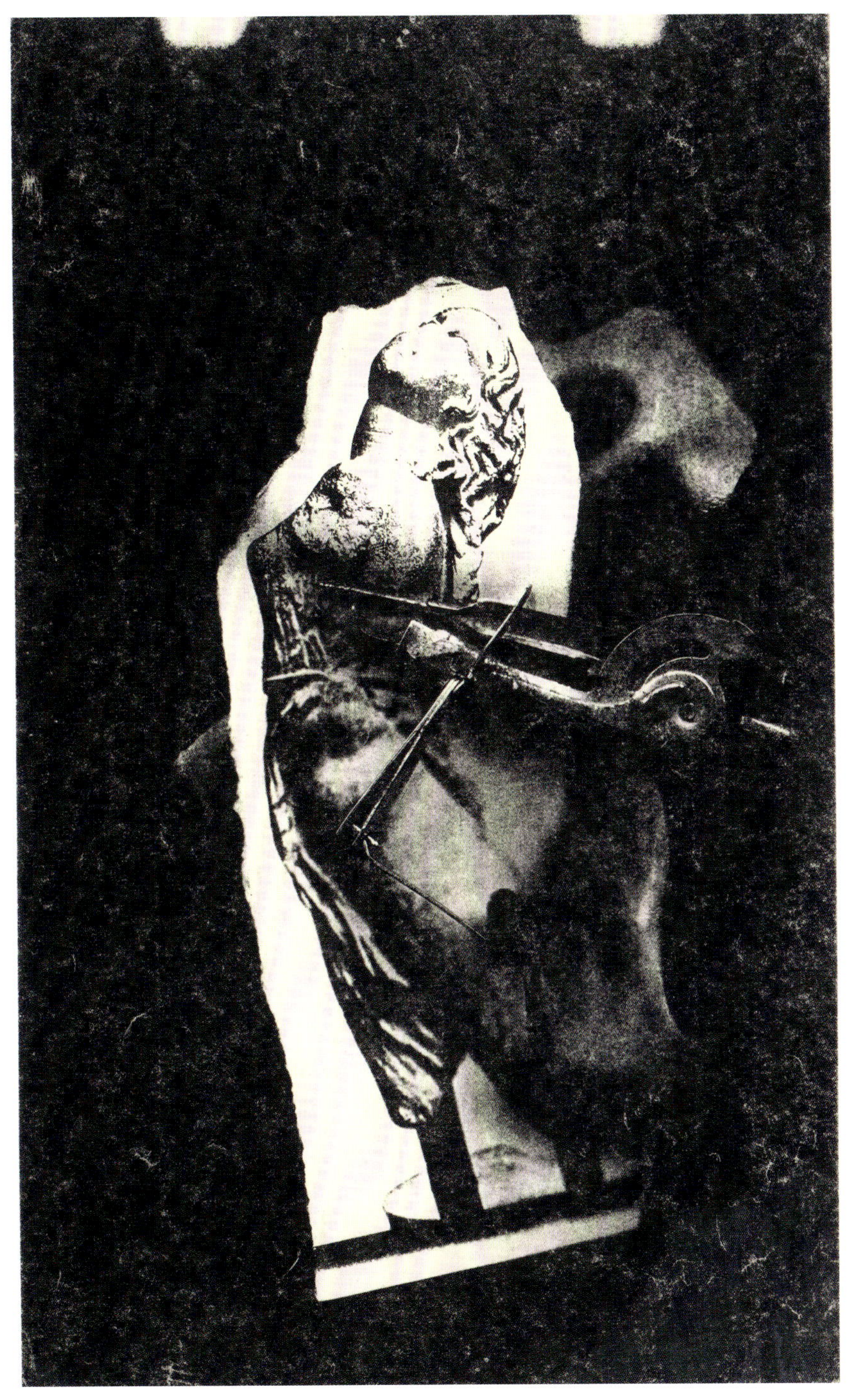

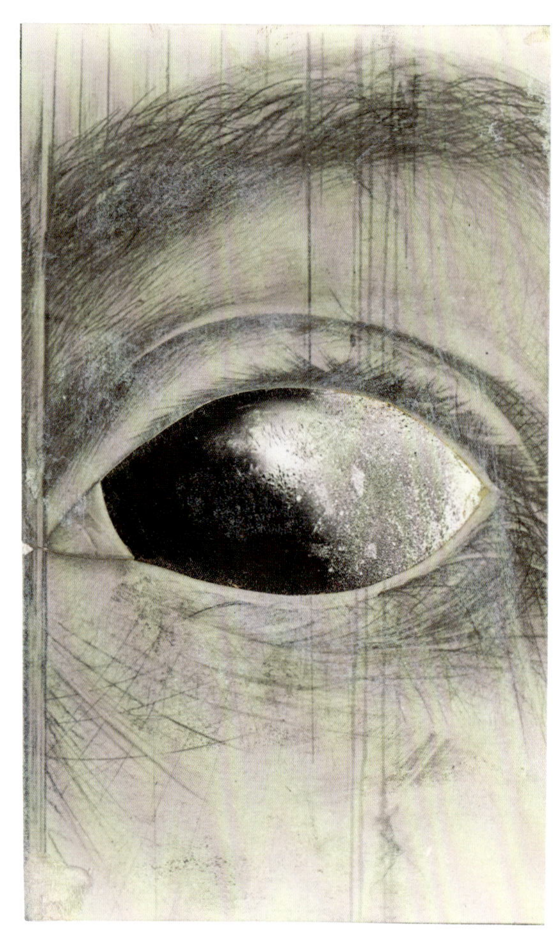

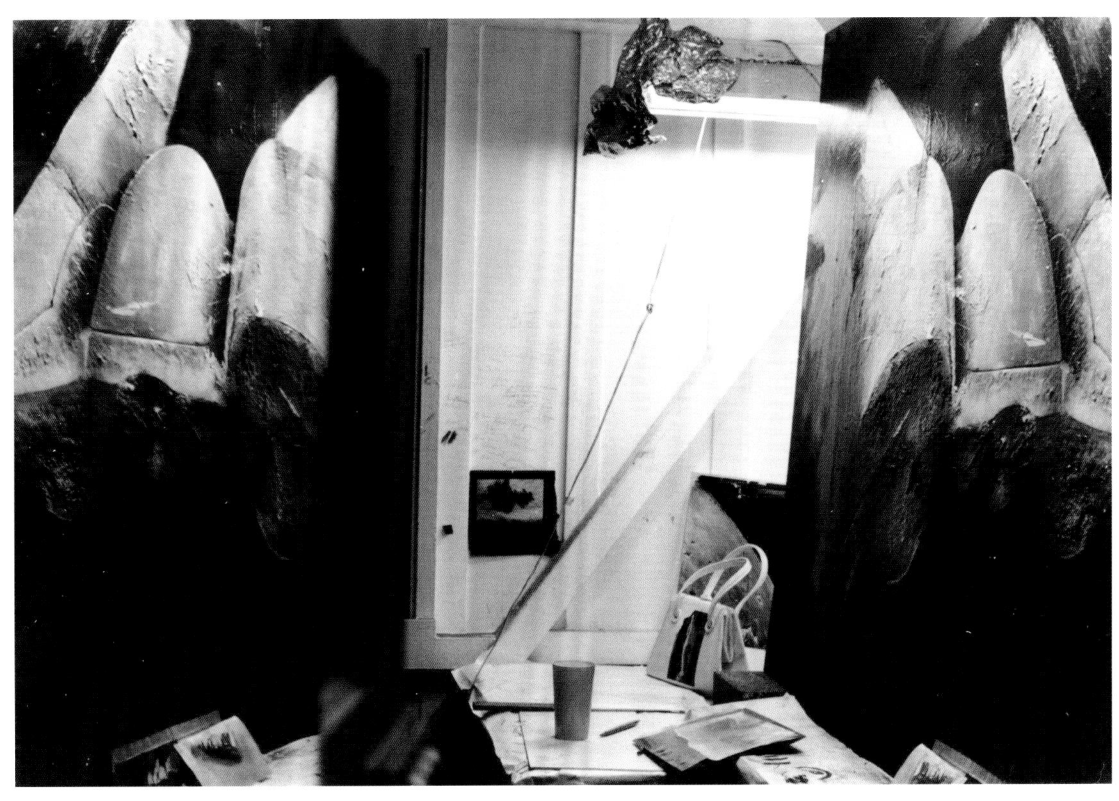

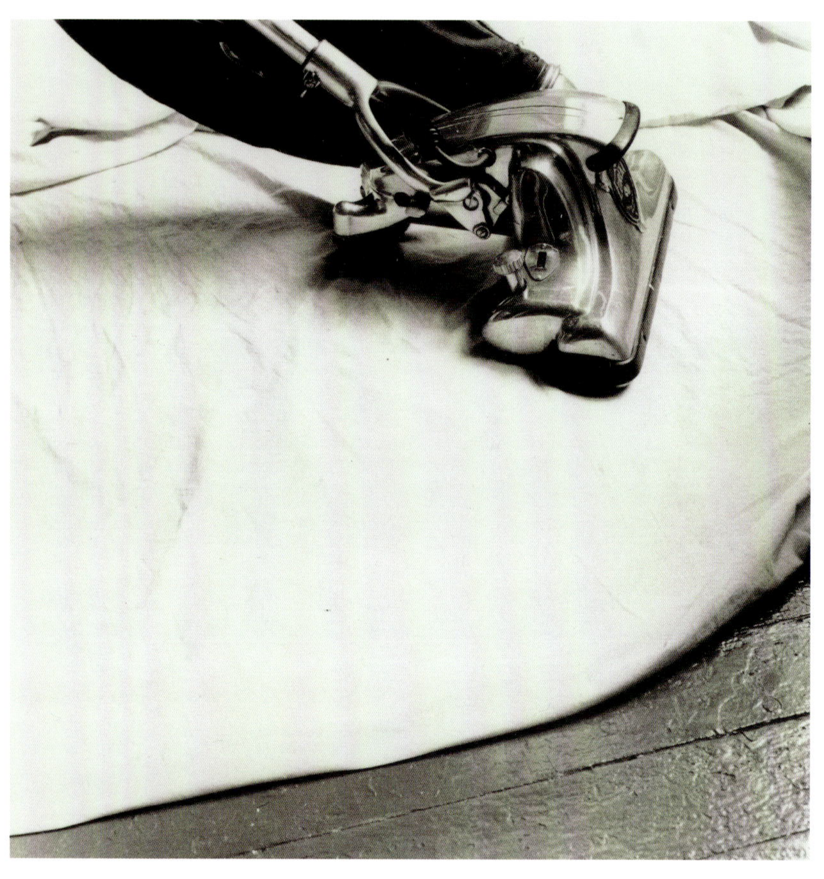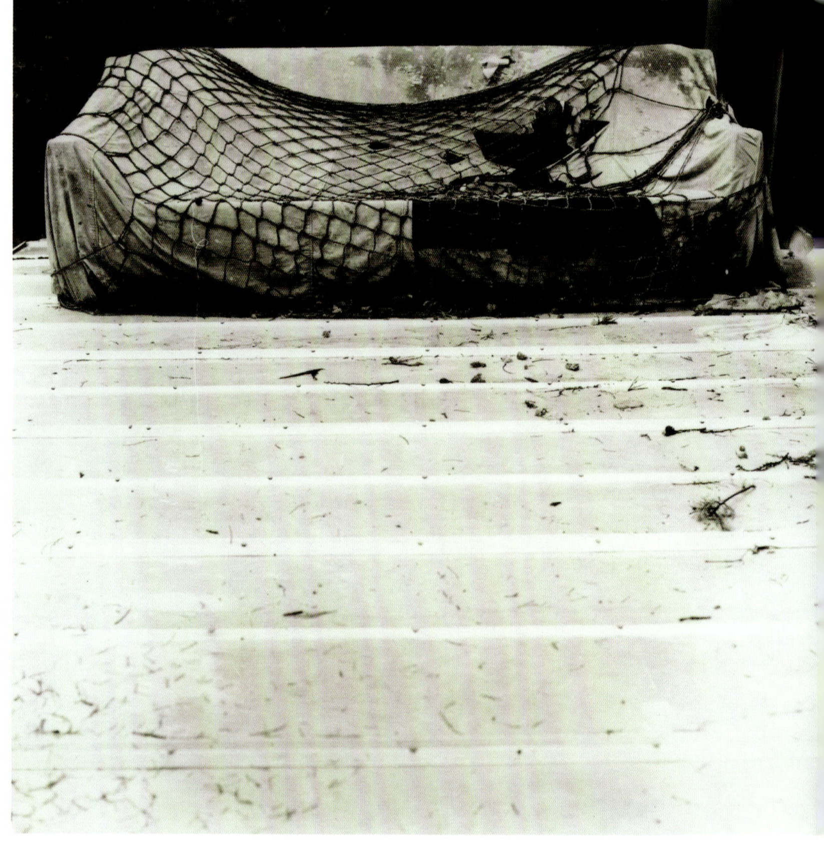

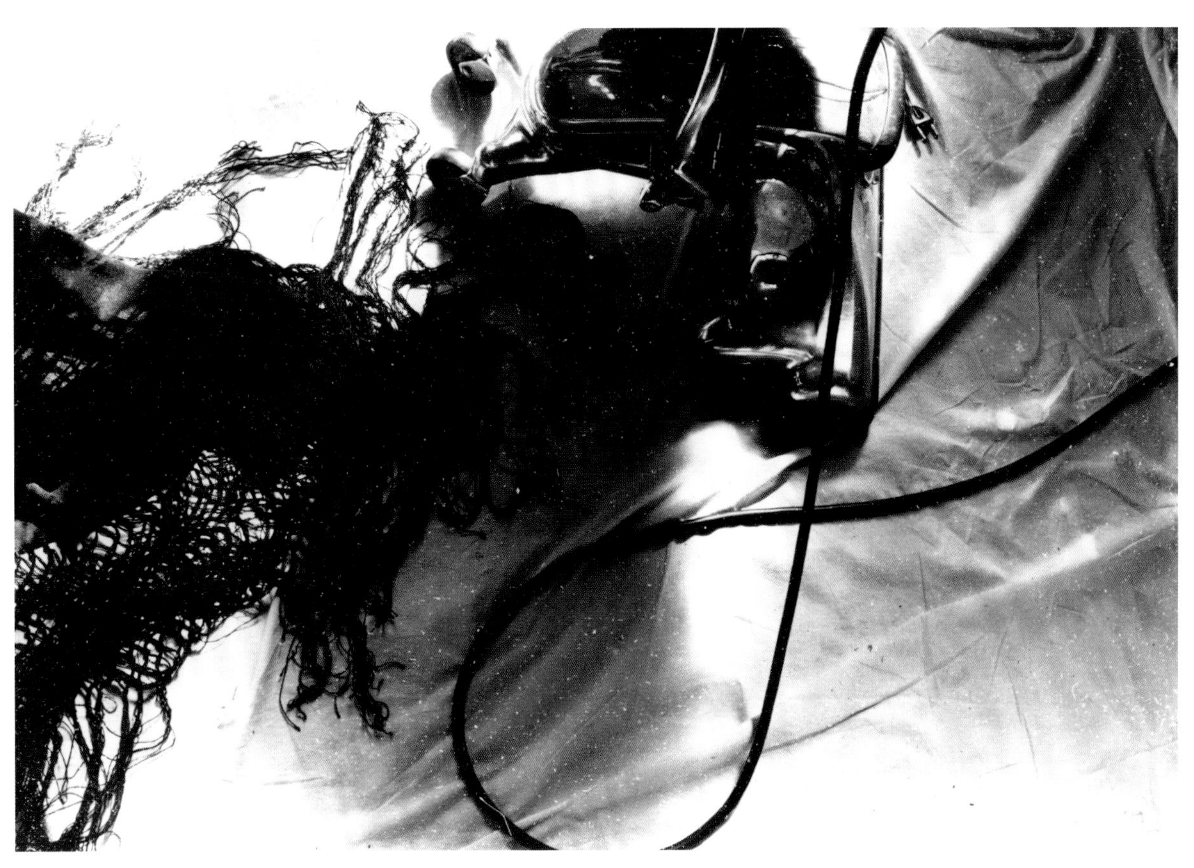

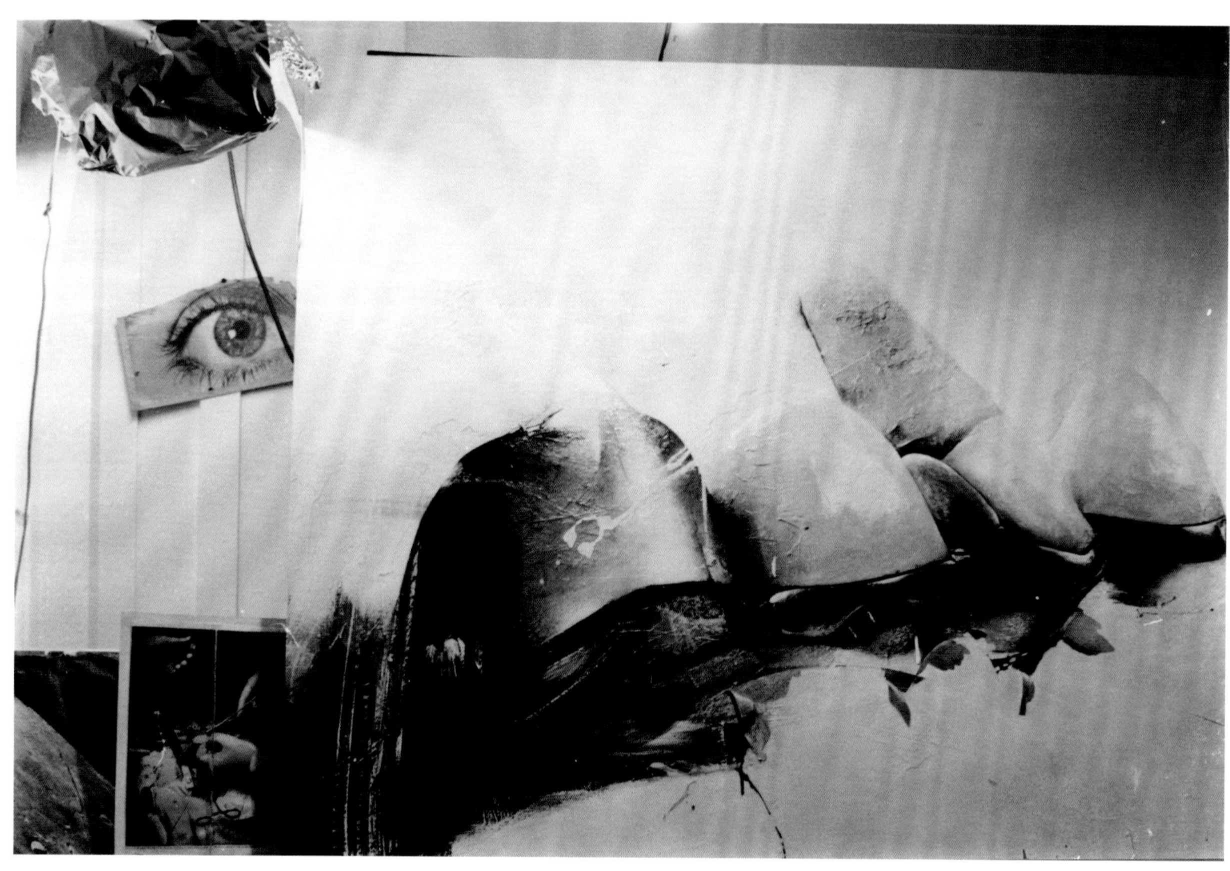

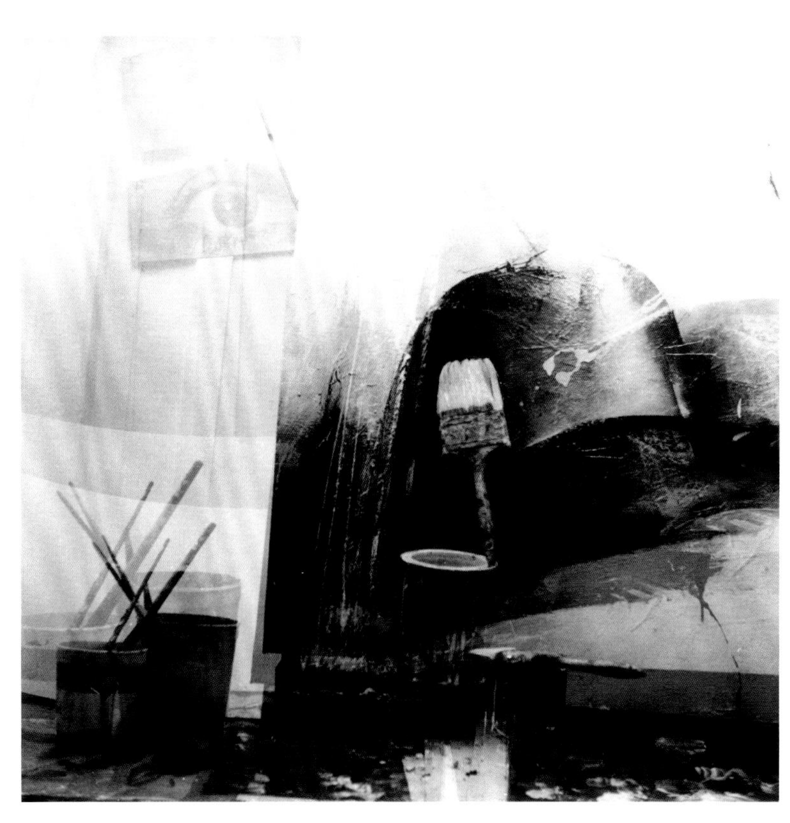

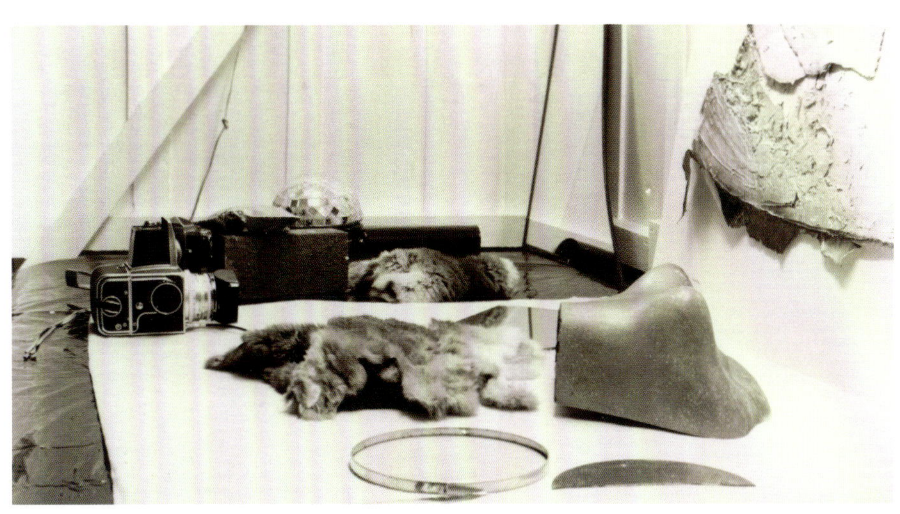

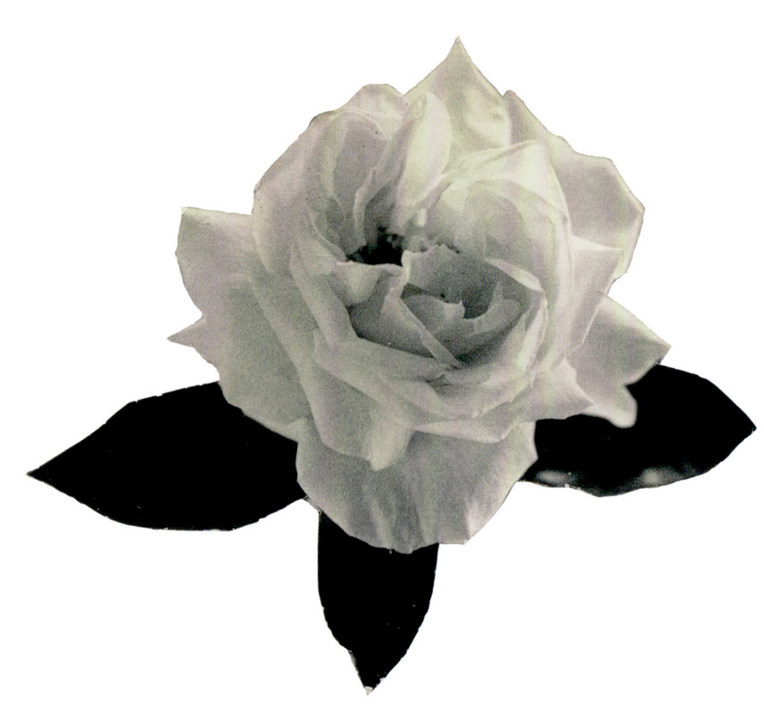

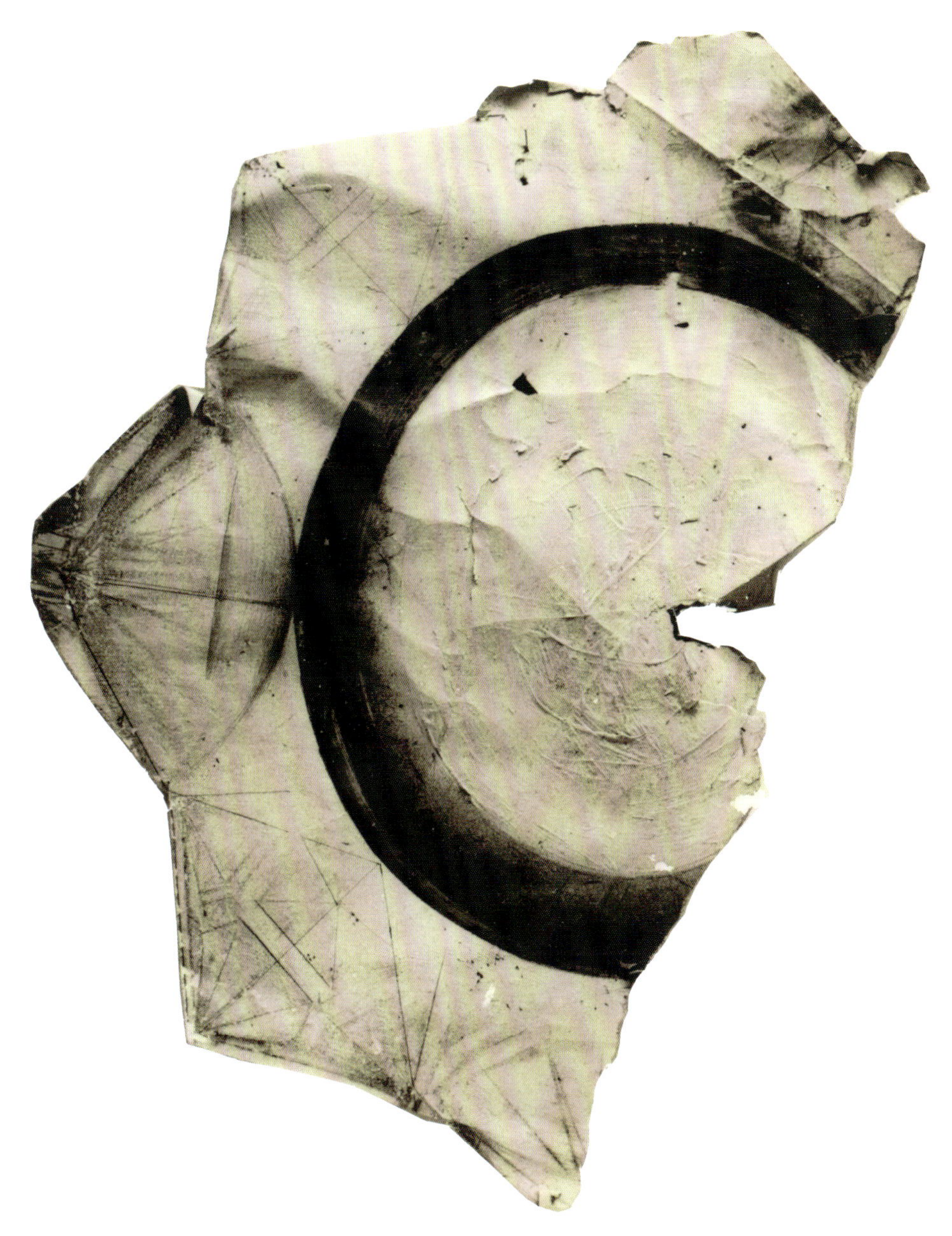

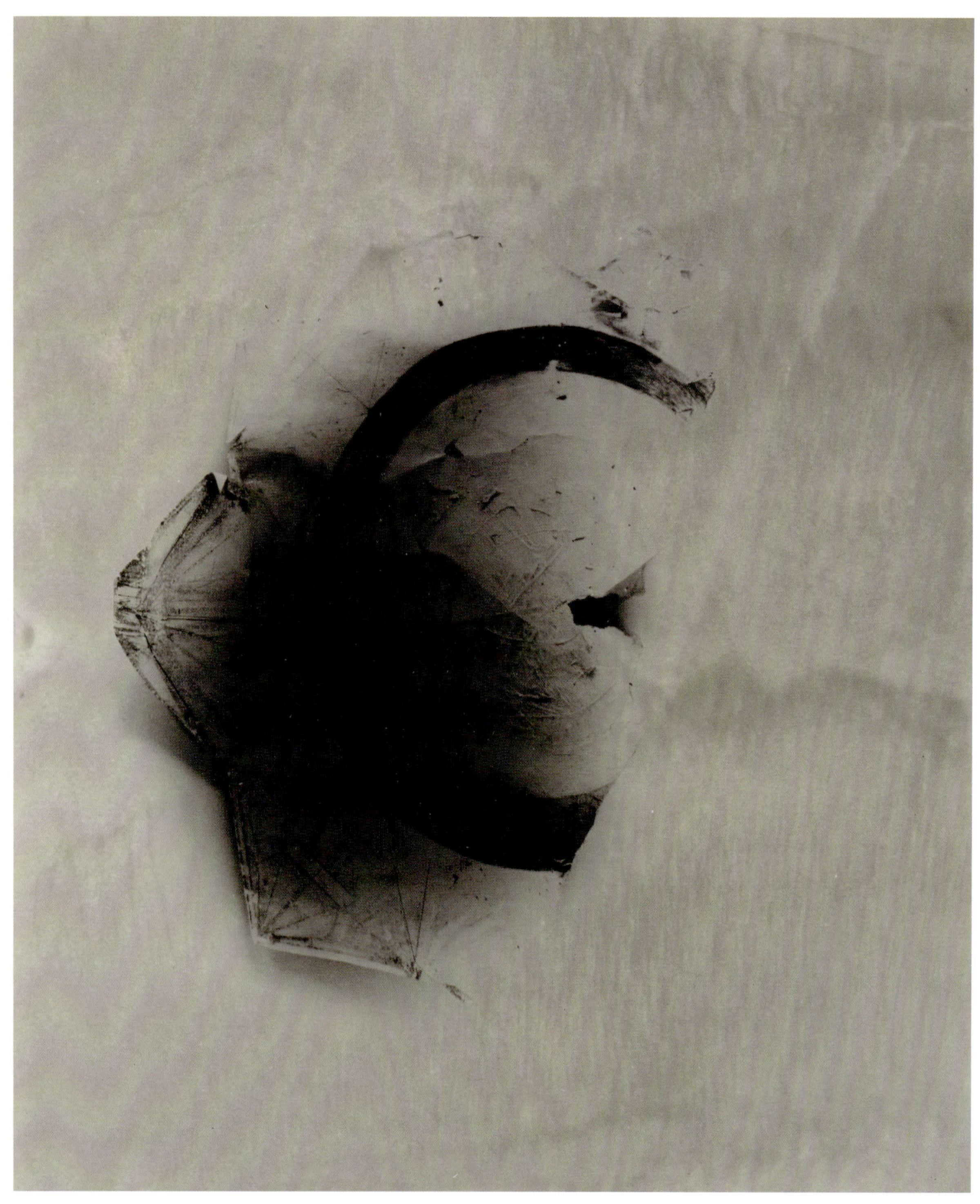

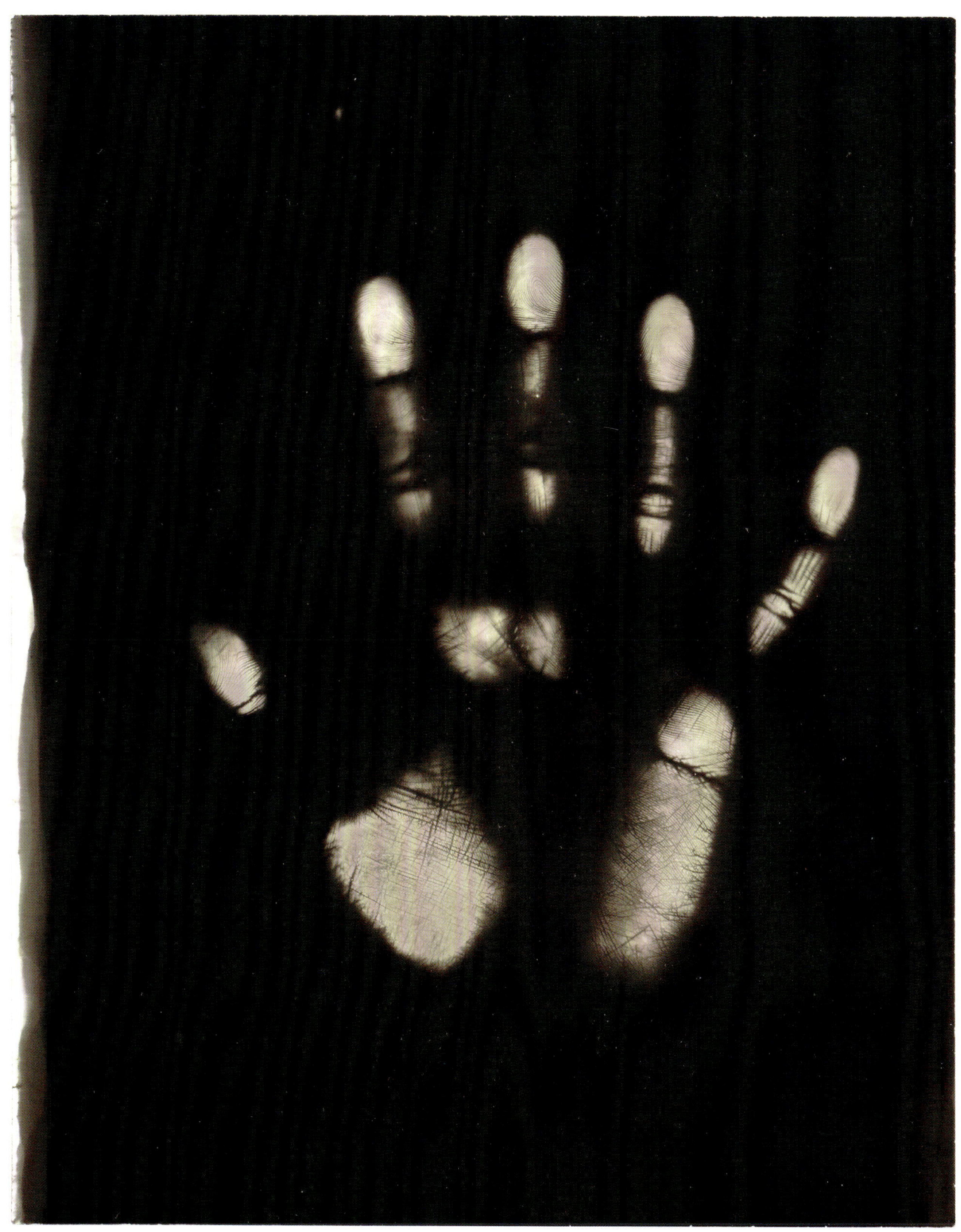

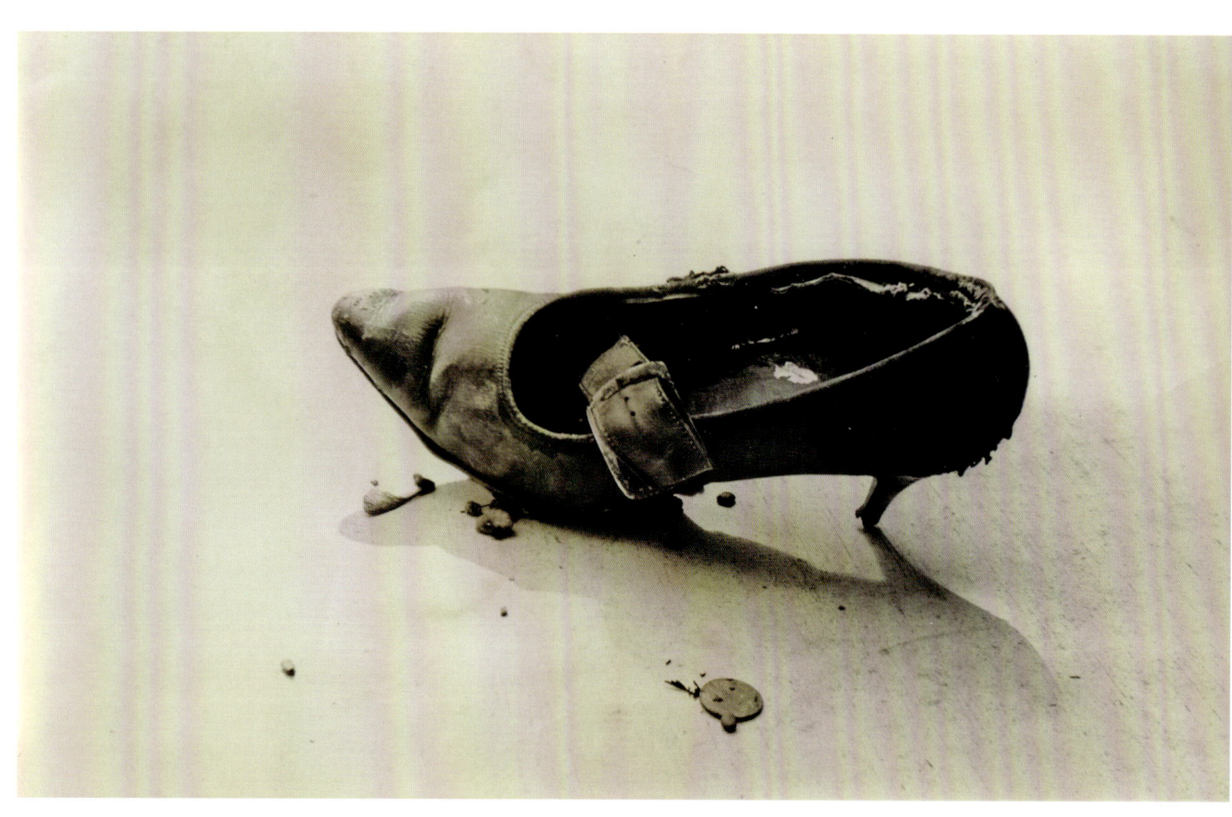

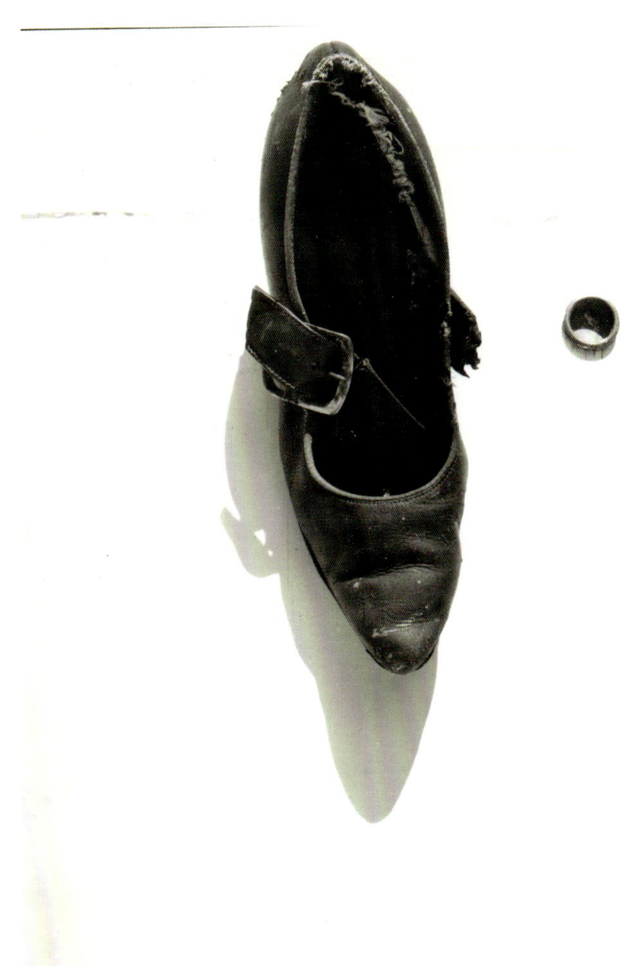

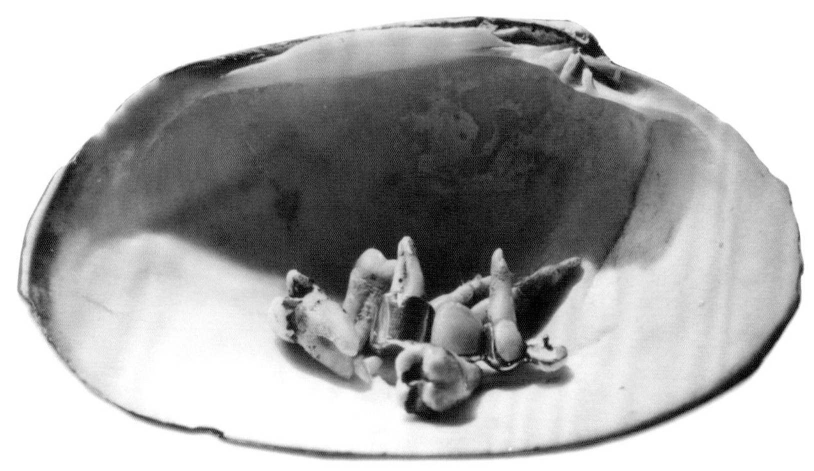

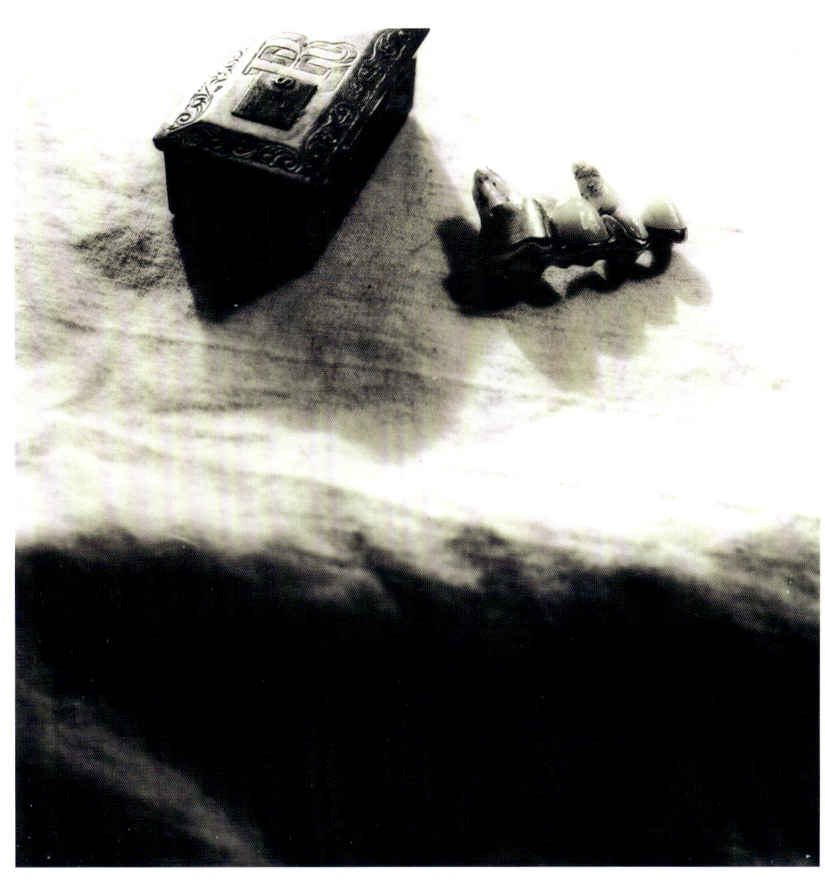

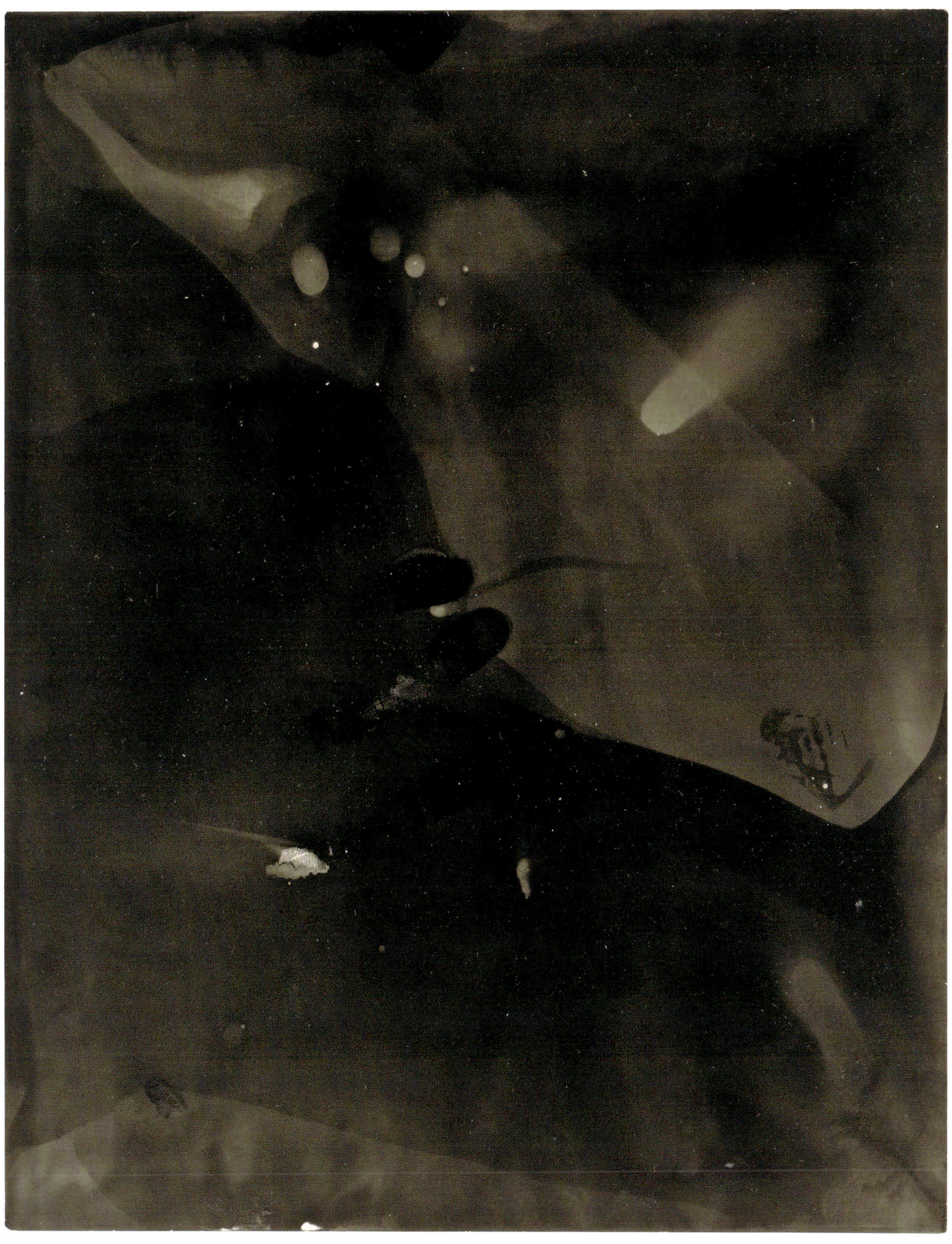

List of Works

2   *Untitled*, 1976
collage of photomechanical
reproduction, gelatin silver print, and
transparent pressure-sensitive tape
9 9/16 × 4 inches (24.3 × 10.2 cm)
Estate no. E2933

5   *Traveling Portrait (Chance Landscape)*,
1973
photo collage with acrylic and glue on
paperboard
14 1/2 × 19 inches (36.8 × 48.3 cm)
Estate no. E2352

25   *Landscape with Figure*, 1955
oil on canvas
18 × 14 inches (45.7 × 35.6 cm)
Estate no. E2798

27   *Still Life*, c. 1955
oil on canvas with fabric, beads, and
thread
25 1/4 × 19 inches (64.1 × 48.3 cm)
Estate no. E2348

29   *Chiaro*, 1985
oil and enamel on paper
50 × 38 inches (127 × 96.5 cm)
Estate no. E1037

31   *White Knight*, 1977
acrylic, graphite, and charcoal with
staple holes on paper
39 7/8 × 30 3/8 inches (101.3 × 77.2 cm)
Estate no. E1451

33   *The Assignment*, 1983
oil and charcoal on linen
66 × 48 inches (167.6 × 121.9 cm)
Estate no. E1318

34–35 *Bride*, 1986
oil on paper mounted on canvas
59 1/4 × 80 1/2 inches (150.5 × 204.5 cm)
Estate no. E1040

36–37 *Untitled (Reclining Figure)*, 1986
oil on paper mounted on canvas
59 3/16 × 80 5/8 inches (150.3 × 204.8 cm)
Estate no. E1314

38   *Untitled*, c. 1959–60
photo collage with typed label, tape,
and offset-printed cardboard on board
7 3/8 × 5 3/4 inches (18.7 × 14.6 cm)
Estate no. E2731

39   *Untitled*, 1973
gelatin silver print
7 1/2 × 9 1/2 inches (19.1 × 24.1 cm)
Estate no. P1320A

40   *Untitled (for B.C.)*, 1973
photo collage on mat board
9 3/4 × 7 3/4 inches (24.8 × 19.7 cm)
Estate no. E1330

41   *Untitled*, 1973
photo collage on paper
11 7/8 × 9 inches (30.2 × 22.9 cm)
Estate no. E3292

42   *Untitled [Human Interest Photo]*, 1973
gelatin silver print
6 1/8 × 6 inches (15.6 × 15.2 cm)
Estate no. P1568B

43   *Untitled*, 1973
gelatin silver print
4 1/2 × 6 5/8 inches (11.4 × 16.8 cm)
Estate no. P0453A

44   *Untitled*, 1973
gelatin silver print
4 1/2 × 4 1/2 inches (11.4 × 11.4 cm)
Estate no. P0511B

45   *Untitled*, 1973
photo collage
8 1/2 × 5 1/2 inches (21.6 × 14 cm)
Estate no. E1555

46   *Untitled*, c. 1975–76
collage of photomechanical
reproduction, gelatin silver print, and
transparent pressure-sensitive tape
8 13/16 × 4 inches (22.4 × 10.2 cm)
Estate no. E2943

47   *Untitled*, c. 1975–76
collage of photomechanical
reproduction, gelatin silver print, and
transparent pressure-sensitive tape
9 1/2 × 4 inches (24.1 × 10.2 cm)
Estate no. E2941

49   *Untitled*, 1975
gelatin silver print
5 1/4 × 4 13/16 inches (13.3 × 12.2 cm)
Estate no. P1479E

50   *Untitled*, 1972
gelatin silver print
3 1/8 × 4 3/4 inches (7.9 × 12.1 cm)
Estate no. P1323A

51   *Untitled*, 1972
cut gelatin silver print
4 3/4 × 5 inches (12.1 × 12.7 cm)
Estate no. P0309

52   *Untitled*, 1973
photo collage
8 3/8 × 8 inches (21.3 × 20.3 cm)
Estate no. E2328

53   *Untitled*, 1974
photo collage
4 11/16 × 4 5/8 inches (11.9 × 11.7 cm)
Estate no. E2334

54   *Untitled*, 1972
gelatin silver print
4 1/8 × 2 13/16 inches (10.5 × 7.1 cm)
Estate no. P0079

      Untitled, 1972
gelatin silver print
4 1/8 × 2 13/16 inches (10.5 × 7.1 cm)
Estate no. P0102

55 *Untitled*, 1974
gelatin silver print
2 ¹⁵⁄₁₆ × 5 ⅛ inches (7.5 × 13 cm)
Estate no. P0965

56 *Untitled*, 1972
gelatin silver print
4 ⁵⁄₁₆ × 2 ¹⁵⁄₁₆ inches (11 × 7.5 cm)
Estate no. P0124

57 *Untitled*, 1974
gelatin silver print
5 ¼ × 4 ¹¹⁄₁₆ inches (13.3 × 11.9 cm)
Estate no. P0517B

58 *Untitled*, 1972
gelatin silver print
2 ¹⁵⁄₁₆ × 4 ⁵⁄₁₆ inches (7.5 × 11 cm)
Estate no. P0215B

59 *Untitled*, 1972
photo collage
4 ⅛ × 5 ¾ inches (10.5 × 14.6 cm)
Estate no. E2309

60 *Untitled*, 1973
gelatin silver print
4 ⅝ × 4 ⅝ inches (11.7 × 11.7 cm)
Estate no. P0364A

61 *Untitled*, 1973
gelatin silver print
4 × 4 inches (10.2 × 10.2 cm)
Estate no. P0502

62–63 *Untitled (R. Mutt's cast)*, 1973
gelatin silver print
4 ⅝ × 3 ½ inches (11.7 × 8.9 cm)
each of six images
Estate no. P1803

64 *Untitled* (*Bone* series), 1975
graphite, ink, and acrylic on paper
10 ¹⁵⁄₁₆ × 8 ½ inches (27.8 × 21.6 cm)
Estate no. E2865

65 *Untitled* (*Bone* series), 1975
graphite and acrylic with cutout
collage on paper
11 × 8 ½ inches (27.9 × 21.6 cm)
Estate no. E1934

66 *Untitled* (*Tripod* series), 1975
graphite and acrylic on paper, cut to
the outline of the figure and laid down
on paper
14 × 11 inches (35.6 × 27.9 cm)
Estate no. E1191

67 *Untitled*, 1976
ink, graphite, and oil pastel with
gelatin silver print on newsprint
11 ¹⁵⁄₁₆ × 9 inches (30.3 × 22.9 cm)
Estate no. E2384

68 *Untitled (for B.C.)*, 1973–74
photo collage
7 ¾ × 4 ³⁄₁₆ inches (19.7 × 10.6 cm)
Estate no. E1327

69 *Untitled*, 1974
graphite, charcoal, and acrylic on rag
board
8 × 7 inches (20.3 × 17.8 cm)
Estate no. E1734

70 *Untitled* (*Bone* series), 1975
graphite and acrylic on cut paper
8 ¾ × 7 inches (22.2 × 17.8 cm)
Estate no. E2060

71 *Untitled*, 1976
gelatin silver print, photomechanical
reproduction, black gesso on cutout
paper, and tape on verso of drawing
pad cover
17 ⅜ × 14 inches (44.1 × 35.6 cm)
Estate no. E3275

72 *Untitled* (*Minnie* series), 1981
graphite on paper
13 ⅝ × 11 inches (34.6 × 27.9 cm)
Estate no. E1467

73 *Study for Bride*, 1986
charcoal and oil pastel on paper
9 × 12 ¹⁄₁₆ inches (22.9 × 30.6 cm)
Estate no. E2713

74 *Untitled* (*Eraser* series), 1979
graphite and charcoal on paper
14 × 11 ¹⁄₁₆ inches (35.6 × 28.1 cm)
Estate no. E1895

75 *Study for Bride*, 1986
ink, oil pastel, charcoal, and sepia ink
on paper
26 ¼ × 39 ⅞ inches (66.7 × 101.3 cm)
Estate no. E2714

76 *Untitled*, 1973
cut gelatin silver print with acrylic on
mat board
3 ¹⁄₁₆ × 3 ³⁄₁₆ inches (7.8 × 8.1 cm)
Estate no. P1576

77 *Trap*, 1972
acrylic and graphite with collage on
Masonite
25 × 22 ¾ inches (63.5 × 57.8 cm)
Estate no. E1321

79 *Untitled*, 1970
acrylic on paper
10 ⁷⁄₁₆ × 15 ³⁄₁₆ inches (26.5 × 38.6 cm)
Estate no. E2351

80 *Untitled*, 1972
gelatin silver print
3 × 4 ⅜ inches (7.6 × 11.1 cm)
Estate no. P0957B

81 *Untitled*, 1972
gelatin silver print
3 × 4 ⅞ inches (7.6 × 12.4 cm)
Estate no. P0352C

82 *Untitled*, 1972
cut gelatin silver print
4 ⅞ × 4 inches (12.4 × 10.2 cm)
Estate no. P0988

83 *Untitled*, 1972
gelatin silver print
4 × 3 ¾ inches (10.2 × 9.5 cm)
Estate no. P1031C

Untitled, 1971
gelatin silver print
2 ⅞ × 4 ⅝ inches (7.3 × 11.7 cm)
Estate no. P1021C

85 *Wings No. 1* (*Angel* series), 1976
ink and tape with collage on paper
14 × 11 inches (35.6 × 27.9 cm)
Estate no. E2867

86 *Untitled*, 1976
gelatin silver print, black paper, pin,
and tape on paper
11 × 8 ½ inches (27.9 × 21.6 cm)
Estate no. E3200

87 *Untitled*, c. 1976
photocopy
11 × 8 ½ inches (27.9 × 21.6 cm)
Estate no. E3330

88 *Untitled*, 1979
photocopy
14 × 8 ½ inches (35.6 × 21.6 cm)
Estate no. E2996

89 *Untitled*, 1979
photocopy
17 × 11 inches (43.2 × 27.9 cm)
Estate no. E3010

90 *Untitled*, 1979
photocopy
14 × 8 ½ inches (35.6 × 21.6 cm)
Estate no. E2994

    Untitled, 1979
photocopy
14 × 8 ½ inches (35.6 × 21.6 cm)
Estate no. E2989

91 *Untitled*, 1979
photocopy
14 × 8 ½ inches (35.6 × 21.6 cm)
Estate no. E2990

92 *Untitled*, c. 1972
photo collage
4 ¾ × 2 ⅞ inches (12.1 × 7.3 cm)
Estate no. E3295

93 *Untitled*, 1973
gelatin silver print
4 × 5 ¹⁵⁄₁₆ inches (10.2 × 15.1 cm)
Estate no. P1020C

94 *Untitled*, 1973
gelatin silver print
4 ½ × 4 ½ inches (11.4 × 11.4 cm)
Estate no. P0640A

Untitled, 1973
gelatin silver print
4 ½ × 4 ½ inches (11.4 × 11.4 cm)
Estate no. P0496E

95 *Untitled*, 1973
gelatin silver print
4 ¼ × 6 ¼ inches (10.8 × 15.9 cm)
Estate no. P0641A

96 *Untitled*, 1971
gelatin silver print
4 ⁵⁄₁₆ × 6 ⅜ inches (11 × 16.2 cm)
Estate no. P1607

97 *Untitled*, 1971
gelatin silver print
4 × 4 ⅛ inches (10.2 × 10.5 cm)
Estate no. P1012D

99 *Untitled*, 1973
gelatin silver print
2 ½ × 4 ¾ inches (6.4 × 12.1 cm)
Estate no. P1503B

100 *Untitled*, 1973
cut gelatin silver print
3 ½ × 4 inches (8.9 × 10.2 cm)
Estate no. P0408C

101 *Untitled* (*White Spica*), 1973
cut gelatin silver print
6 ⅜ × 4 ⅜ inches (16.2 × 11.1 cm)
Estate no. P0784J

102 *Untitled* (*White Spica*), 1973
gelatin silver print
8 ¾ × 7 ⅜ inches (22.2 × 18.7 cm)
Estate no. P1527

103 *Untitled*, 1973
gelatin silver print chemigram
9 ¹⁵⁄₁₆ × 8 inches (25.2 × 20.3 cm)
Estate no. P0540

104 *Untitled*, 1973
gelatin silver print
4 ¾ × 7 ¾ inches (12.1 × 19.7 cm)
Estate no. P0605A

105 *Untitled*, 1973
gelatin silver print
5 ⁵⁄₁₆ × 5 inches (13.5 × 12.7 cm)
Estate no. P0607A

106 *Untitled*, 1973
cut gelatin silver print
2 ⅜ × 4 ¼ inches (6 × 10.8 cm)
Estate no. P0990E

107 *Untitled*, 1973
gelatin silver print
4 × 4 inches (10.2 × 10.2 cm)
Estate no. P1001I

109 *Untitled* (*Salvador Dalí's Birthday Party*),
1973
gelatin silver print chemigram
9 ¹⁵⁄₁₆ × 7 ¹⁵⁄₁₆ inches (25.2 × 20.2 cm)
Estate no. P0542

This catalogue was published on the occasion
of the exhibition:

**Outrageous Fortune:
Jay DeFeo and Surrealism**

March 1–April 7, 2018

Mitchell-Innes & Nash
534 West 26th Street
New York, NY 10001
212 744 7400 miandn.com

Publication © 2018 Mitchell-Innes & Nash
Essay © 2018 Dana Miller
All artwork © 2018 The Jay DeFeo
Foundation / Artists Rights Society (ARS),
New York

Design: Matthew Polhamus
Printing: Phoenix Litho, Philadelphia
Publication Director: Cassandra Lozano
with Kevin Choe
Photography: Benjamin Blackwell
Copy Editor: Anna Drozda

Front cover: *Untitled*, 1976
Back cover: *Untitled*, 1974

All rights reserved. No part of this
publication may be used or reproduced,
in whole or in part, including illustrations,
in any manner whatsoever without written
permission from the copyright holders.

ISBN: 978-0-9986312-3-3

Available through
ARTBOOK | D.A.P.
75 Broad Street, Suite 630
New York, NY 10004
212 627 1999 artbook.com

Dana Miller wishes to acknowledge the
important assistance she received from
Leah Levy, Michael Carr, and Dawn Troy
of The Jay DeFeo Foundation, as well as
Cassandra Lozano from Mitchell-Innes
& Nash.

The Jay DeFeo Foundation wishes to
thank Lucy Mitchell-Innes and David
Nash, as well as Tymberly Canale, Kevin
Choe, Lucy Dew, Elizabeth DiSabatino,
Robert Grosman, Isabelle Hogenkamp,
Jeffrey Horne, Cassandra Lozano, Sheldon
Mukamal, Isobel Nash, Josephine Nash,
Peter Tecu, and Courtney Willis Blair at
Mitchell-Innes & Nash; and Dana Miller
for her insightful essay.